PRAISE FOR
Revved! Obsessions of a Midlife Motorcyclist . . .

"A brilliantly written, accurate tale of the life of a returning rider who also happens to be a scholar. His is an entertaining book, unique in the genre, that captures the rider's mind, aspirations, and passion while giving more than a few good pointers too. Mr. Kirk's writing is transformative, sobering yet jocular, and always enticing. Read this book!"

—**Will Guyan,** moto journalist and editor of
On The Level BMW Magazine

"*Revved!* tells the captivating story of a rider's quest for mastery despite his fears and anxieties. Kirk's personal account in 'Terrors of the Track' describes, with humor and insight, how his enrollment in *CLASS* highlighted and helped him deal with those fears and begin his advancement as a skilled rider. I highly recommend this journey into the world of motorcycling."

—**Reg Pridmore,** three-time AMA Superbike
champion, member of AMA Hall of Fame, and
founder of CLASS Motorcycle School

"I enjoyed this ramble through Kirk's riding life as it paralleled my own so closely. As I read the book, I seemed to converse with the author all afternoon in a pleasantly unexpected way. It is a well-written book with a focus on the long-range as well as close details of a rider's life. I felt as though I was riding on the back of the author's bike."

"Stuart Kirk elegantly puts into language what we fellow riders perhaps only know viscerally—what it means to become proficient and 'one with our machines.' As a recognized scholar on mental health, Kirk's stories reinforce the adage that you never see a motorcycle parked in front of a psychiatrist's office."

"Stuart Kirk is, quite simply, a wonderful writer. His reflections on twenty-five years of motorcycling draw the reader into a vivid, richly detailed world. More than a story about riding a motorcycle, these tales have much to tell us about what it means to be human—about facing one's fears, opening oneself to unexpected companions, and trusting the unknown road ahead. As Kirk shows us, it really *is* about the journey, not the destination."

"This entertaining and well-written book is the perfect concise guide to the motorcycling experience for auto lovers and others who know little about the world of motorcycles. Kirk's sometimes poetic reflections introduce us to a diverse community of riders and the reasons they ride, the bikes they ride, the gear they must wear, the rides they take, and the pleasures and risks of motorcycling. Both informative and delightful to read."

—**Ted Benjamin,** retired professor of social policy, UCLA

"*Revved!* is an enjoyable read. It covers many miles and subjects—even delightfully controversial ones like lane splitting, double yellows, and speed—as well as mysteries such as counter-steering, which was not a known concept when I learned to ride sixty years ago."

—**Clement Salvadori,** author of *No Thru Road* and columnist for *Rider*

"This wonderful and well-written moto memoir gives full vent to the pleasures of midlife cruising alone and with others. It stimulates the reader's self-examination of their own wanderlust and love affair with biking and may trigger others to buy a bike and ride."

—**Tomi Gomory,** Fulbright scholar, Florida State University

"*Revved!* describes in uncanny detail the inner experience of motorcycling that is ever present but often ignored because it lies right at the edge of awareness—the fears and the thrills, the vulnerabilities and the triumphs, the solitary moments and the shared joys. It's as though Kirk was inside my head narrating the total experience for me, helping me appreciate even more the sublime excitement and ecstasy of riding."

—**Wally Gingerich,** professor emeritus, Case Western Reserve University, and an avid adventure motorcyclist

"*Revved!* conveys the joys of motorcycling through the art of storytelling rather than teaching and preaching. Kirk's humility of starting to ride in mid-life and reaching proficiency through passion and persistence allows each of us to relive similar struggles in our lives with humor and compassion. I found myself relating to every page."

—**Frances Sayre,** co-owner of OCD Custom Cycles & Auto Repair, Santa Fe

"'So *that's* what it's all about. Now I get it!' A fast read and fast ride to the insights of motorcycling and the obsessions therein."

—**Karen Roberts,** wife of a midlife motorcyclist

"I found myself smiling with fond memories as I followed Dr. Kirk's evolution from an occasional rider to a full-fledged addict. There is plenty here for nonriders as well, who will gain much insight into the minds of those two-wheeled wackos with whom they share the roads."
—**Michael Banister,** facilities manager

"Captivating, provocative, and courageously transparent. *Revved!* brilliantly portrays the romance and pleasures of journeying through life on two wheels."
—**Florian Neuhauser,** managing editor, *RoadRUNNER Motorcycle Touring & Travel*

"Stuart Kirk has penned a terrific book that is bound to become a classic in the annals of motorcycling. The work is all the more notable given that the author suffers from a debilitating condition of motorcycle addiction. Read on and ride on."
—**Robert Schilling,** professor, Luskin School of Public Affairs, UCLA, and motorcyclist

"A vivid and delightful account. *Revved!* is a window onto the world of motorcycling and a meditation on the joy of becoming more than you expected."
—**Heather W. Huffman,** EdM, PhD, cultural anthropologist, Colorado Outdoor Education Center

Ride far, be safe,
enjoy the journey.

Stuart G K_____

Revved!

Nothing behind me,
everything ahead of me,
as is ever so on the road.

—JACK KEROUAC, *ON THE ROAD*

Revved!

Obsessions of a
Midlife Motorcyclist

Stuart A. Kirk

Corkscrew
PUBLISHING

Santa Fe, New Mexico

Published by: Corkscrew Publishing
            36 Camino De Los Montoyas
            Santa Fe, NM 87506
            www.corkscrewpublishing.com

Editors: Ann Mason, Ellen Kleiner
Book design and production: Ann Lowe
Cover photo: Pascal Pierme (pascalpierme.com)

The essays entitled "Crash Landing" and "Twisty Knot" were originally
published in a slightly different form in *BMW Owners News*; an earlier
version of "Crash Landing" was also published in *CityBike*.

Printed in the United States of America

Publisher's Cataloging-in-Publication Data

Kirk, Stuart A., 1945-

   Revved! : obsessions of a midlife motorcyclist / Stuart A. Kirk. -- Santa
   Fe, New Mexico : Corkscrew Publishing, [2016]

      pages ; cm.

      ISBN: 978-0-9963896-0-0 (pbk.) ; 978-0-9963896-1-7 (ebook)
      Summary: A midcareer professor unexpectedly becomes immersed in
   the world of sport motorcycling. The book describes his challenges and
   triumphs in mastering the skills of riding.--Publisher.

GV1060.2.K47 A3 2016   2015941059
796.7/5092—dc23   1601

1 3 5 7 9 10 8 6 4 2

To all my riding companions
over the past twenty-five years

ACKNOWLEDGMENTS

I would like to express my gratitude to some of the many people who assisted in the creation of this book. Drafts of my very first essays were patiently reviewed by my nonriding friend Karen Staller, who encouraged my attempts to write about motorcycling and offered sage advice about how to find my voice and write more effectively. My wife, Carol Ann, who has graced my life through all these motorcycling years and lovingly supported my riding lifestyle, has always served as my first reader. She is responsible for making this book more succinct and much better. Also, following the pathway of less is more, my energetic editors, Ann Mason and Ellen Kleiner in Santa Fe, enormously improved the prose and my competent designer, Ann Lowe, laid out and designed this handsome book. If editing and designing were riding, they would be first and most skilled around the next turn.

CONTENTS

Foreword

RIDING IS MUTABLE. Infinite, if you want to get poetic. It is change itself: every second the landscape is rearranged just for you; every second takes you that much deeper into a future quickly becoming past. Changed chemically, until you come out the other side, remade.

Pity the poor souls who never knew bikes. For them, there's *Revved!*

There is only one way to go: the cover stripped off, no mediating force between body and the world's sensuality. What you see through the visor goes straight to the heart in a millisecond of lacerating truth.

Once, every ride was an embarkation to new lands. Giddy expectation attended the predeparture unfurling of maps. Everything was seen for the first time, and firsts are always delicious, even first disasters, first conundrums, first mistakes. Yet you are also on a one-way journey to a place called mid-life. It's a numbers game: ride long enough, live long enough, and the motorcycle trip more often than not becomes a voyage of rediscovery. (*We have all been here before.*) Down every road, you happen upon previous lives, and suddenly the hopes you felt then recur vivid as that burst of cold air by the cement mines on Route 213: a wall of frigidity passed through before you can formulate the thought "That was cold!" In a car this would have been a ghost so faint you would remain unsure it had really touched you. Riding opens your pores.

The rider ahead of me was not aware, dropping speed before the sleepy quarter mile representing the full extent of the Catskills village, that behind him I was twisting in the saddle to look up the mountain clove we had just passed. I wanted to see a part of me. I glimpsed it before I had to face forward again or face a fall: a white farmhouse, reduced against vast mowed fields and encircling woods. The house of a dear friend I had not seen in a decade. And down the road from her, invisible behind the trees, the first house I'd ever owned—into which I brought my son, two days old. Everywhere memories waited in ambush: there, I had pulled over for a yard sale and found a chipped and crazed green plate, beauty deepened by its unknowable history. And there, in that valley, I sat down in a rocky stream one oppressive August day, so miserable in swelled pregnancy I could not drive another mile without relief. An hour later found us on the road that had been my secret possession, where my love for a little white bike grew with each turn, and every season altered the quality of the air and light slanting through green then flared orange then cool brown.

Four hundred miles through the regions of memory. And that was just west. If we'd gone farther, we would have run into my childhood. South, my young adulthood.

Of course, if we'd gone southeast, my riding partner would have ridden through almost the entirety of *his* life, and I would not have known the sight of what backyards and boarded-up buildings would touch him too with nostalgia's pleasant ache. It is a sensation so synesthetic it could only come from cutting the air on a motorcycle, through time's own borders.

When I say this is a numbers game, this riding through a lifetime, I mean it is also a geographical one. In short, time to leave North America, unfold new maps to memories yet unmade. This project makes us new again: we are always young riders in new lands. Going, I will be reborn. Winding roads, unwinding time.

— Melissa Holbrook Pierson

First bike, 1964 Yamaha 80

Preface

MOTORCYCLING IS NOT ONLY an adventurous mode of transportation or a challenging sport; it can also be a passion reflecting a great deal about a person, as it has been for me. This book recounts my experiences rediscovering motorcycling in mid-life; how I developed riding skills and found my niche among motorcyclists; and how aspects of riding reflect my identity, perspective on life, and state of mind. This has been an unanticipated journey into an unforeseen world. Other riders have known at the start what they were pursuing and where it might lead based on having friends or family who were motorcyclists, but I had no such acquaintances, no forewarnings of my involvement in the activity, and no expectations of how profoundly it would ultimately affect my life.

Motorcyclists are people for whom motorcycling, in some of its variegated forms, has become a continuing preoccupation—some might say passion—in their lives. People do not become motorcyclists by simply owning motorcycles. There are thousands of motorcycles neglected in corners of garages that have not been ridden very far. They were acquired because individuals thought they might enjoy riding, but, for whatever reasons, their casual involvement in the world of motorcycling ended early. Such people probably would not identify themselves as motorcyclists. Then there are others who once owned motorcycles but sold them years ago. They might have not liked riding, had no time, needed some extra cash, assumed new family or job responsibilities. For twenty years, I was in this category myself. Although I had owned small Yamaha 80 and Honda 350 motorcycles for several years, I never considered myself a motorcyclist, either then or over the ensuing two decades. But gradually, being a motorcyclist became my foremost identity. Others who are passionate about some aspect of their lives probably experience the same phenomenon. Some avid fishermen, triathletes, and artists, for example, are so preoccupied with their passion that it doesn't merely describe what they do but defines who they are.

This book is not an instructional manual for learning how to ride. Many other people have written books for that purpose, such as David Hough's authoritative *Proficient Motorcycling* or Lawrence Grodsky's *Stayin' Safe*. Nor do I imagine that these essays represent the discoveries of all riders, although I hope other motorcyclists will identify with aspects of my story. Moreover, the book is not a travelogue like Ted Simon's well-known *Jupiter's Travels* or Clement Salvadori's engaging *No Thru Road*. It is not my intent to take readers along on all the roads I've traveled, describe what I saw, where I dined, or where I stayed at night. I also do not guide readers through a philosophical journey, as ably accomplished by others, like Robert Pirsig in *Zen and the Art of Motorcycle Maintenance* and Matthew Crawford in *Shop Class as Soulcraft*. And since I began riding in my forties, I don't convey the adolescent angst and lust so humorously recounted by Jack Riepe in *Conversations with a Motorcycle*. Instead, this book belongs in the genre of personal reflections on the moto life, cultivated skillfully for thirty years by Peter Egan in his columns for *Cycle World* and in *Leanings*, a three-volume collection of his stories and musings. Also in that genre is Melissa Holbrook Pierson's *The Perfect Vehicle*, the story of her immersion in this special world, published about the time I first began writing essays on motorcycling.

During my early years of riding, I had no idea that I would ever write about it. As an author of academic publications, however, I knew that writing helps people think more clearly. Half-baked ideas and shallow understandings usually reveal themselves as we put them on paper for others to read, prompting us to examine our thinking, go deeper into arguments, look carefully at conflicting evidence, and be more self-reflective.

As I became increasingly engrossed in motorcycling, I realized it was a peculiar involvement for a midcareer professor and that it was becoming an obsession, but I didn't know how or why this had happened or where it was leading. The most common question that motorcyclists are asked, "Why do you ride a motorcycle?" always left me struggling to understand the reason for my involvement. Sometimes while rambling incoherently to someone about this I could see their puzzled expression and imagine their eyes rolling as they probably mused to themselves, "Just what I expected—there are no good reasons. He's a risk-taking thrill-seeking maverick."

In fact, it is as difficult to explain why I ride as it is to explain the other choices I've made in life. Among all that we are and do, we usually emphasize a few salient traits that are deeply meaningful to us. When asked by strangers who I am or what I do, I say I am a professor of social welfare at UCLA, now retired. Or, in another context, I might indicate that I am a father and grandfather. If asked, however, *why* I am a professor or father, my answer would entail a more byzantine autobiographical account because such aspirations are folded deep within me and might be fragmented, partially unknown, distorted by selective memories, or filtered by emotions and shaped by unconscious fantasies. All motorcyclists have their own stories about why they ride and what it means to them. Although each story is unique, the common elements that surface may help piece together the jigsaw puzzle of why we all ride.

In writing about my moto life, I hoped that I would get a better handle on what it was that I was experiencing intensively—escape, exhilaration, risk, adventure, and mastery—and why. The essays were written during different stages of my midlife involvement in motorcycling, beginning about five years into it. Twenty-five years and half a million miles later, these are my reflections on how my passion for motorcycling grew over time, and what I have learned about myself and life through motorcycling. Collectively they provide an answer to why I ride.

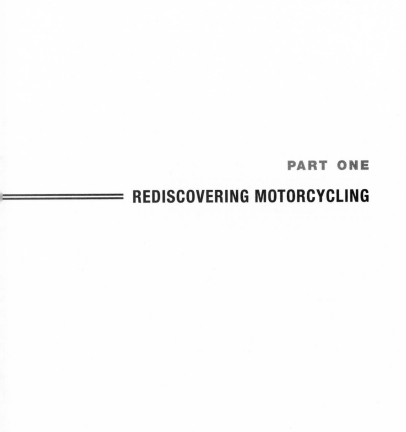

PART ONE

REDISCOVERING MOTORCYCLING

1991 BMW K75S

1. Crash Landing on Reentry

THE SENSATIONS of motorcycling can be intoxicating and, like other intoxicants, dangerous. After rediscovering motorcycling twenty-five years ago, when I was forty-five and hadn't owned a motorcycle for twenty years, just two miles into my very first ride I crashed. This was a traumatic lesson in the need for learning the skills of motorcycling rather than allowing myself to be seduced by its sensations. I hadn't considered owning a motorcycle since I had sold a small Honda in 1972, when I was twenty-five. At that time, I was a graduate student and new father and it seemed like the prudent thing to do. The sale had divorced me from the world of motorcycling for two decades as I pursued an academic career. Then in 1990 while living and teaching in New York City, I rediscovered motorcycling with great anticipation and a little angst.

My reentry began as innocent inspiration when one day I snooped around my neighbor Mike Fitzgibbons's small barn near our weekend house in Upstate New York. Mike, a forty-five-year-old high school teacher, was the kind of guy my wife wished I were, a tradesman and tinkerer who could fix anything. His barn was always full of tires and tractor parts, scraps of wire and wood, a half-built three-wheel car, a small sailboat, and other objects that were either works in progress or junk in wait of a brainstorm. Among the objects in the barn was an old 175cc Yamaha Exciter that had been gathering dust for years. I presume that I had seen it a hundred times, but never had it stimulated any more interest in me than Mike's wheelbarrow. I knew that Mike had once owned motorcycles but hadn't ridden in a decade. And although we were close friends and often discussed such weighty matters as the merits of marriage and divorce, fatherhood, teaching, and the use of tractors and chainsaws, we had never seriously discussed motorcycles.

On this October day, perhaps feeling tremors of middle age, I sat on the small bike for the first time and some distant memories stirred. These were stimulated not by any conscious thought process but by the physical sensation of leaning forward onto handlebars, having my fingers curled around them, and resting my feet on small pegs.

"Mike," I asked without thinking, "when are you going to get this bike running and sell it?" And then, without deliberation, I blurted out, "When you get it running, maybe I'll buy it." It was a casual, irrational statement, the sort of idle verbal nonsense that good friends tolerate from each other.

Although Mike had previously mentioned that he wanted to get rid of the Yamaha, he made it clear that he didn't want to sell it to me. "You don't want that bike," he counseled, "it's too small. It was my ex-wife's bike."

"Yeah, but wouldn't it be fun to ride motorcycles again? It's been a long, long time," I offered.

"That bike won't do. You'll want something bigger," he said, jumping way ahead of me.

"Well," I countered, mischievously, "why don't we buy a couple of bigger motorcycles and do some riding next summer?"

Until uttering those fateful words, I had not entertained such a thought for decades. The words sprung from an unconscious, uncensored corner of my psyche. I expected my reckless proposal to fall on deaf ears. Why, I reasoned, would Mike, a single father responsible for two school-age daughters, or me, who had not ridden in many years or had much expendable cash, need or want to buy a motorcycle?

Nevertheless, that day Mike, perhaps also vulnerable to the tremors of middle age, and I became rebels against rationality, captives of the image of roaming backcountry roads astride motorcycles. Although we both recognized the basic irrationality of the idea, once it had been articulated it was as if the genie had been let out of the bottle, and we were unable to suppress the thought of re-creating the motorcycling memories of our youth. With enthusiasm aroused, we agreed to look at some motorcycles during my next weekend visit. Although I did not know it at the time, sitting in a cluttered barn in Upstate New York mindlessly shooting the breeze with a friend had just altered the course of my life.

In the interest of full disclosure, I must confess that as middle-aged men Mike and I had never really outgrown our adolescent fondness for fine automobiles, and we both owned modestly sporty BMW 300 series cars. So we were naturally interested in exploring the latest in motorcycling technology and inclined to look at BMW motorcycles, affectionately referred to as Beemers. After doing some preliminary research, we quickly discovered how much motorcycling technology had changed over the years. Beemers now had computer-controlled fuel injection, reliable electric starters, antilock disc brakes, and the ergonomics for long-distance travel. Beemers seemed like just what two teachers needed in returning to motorcycling after long sabbaticals.

Consequently, a few weeks later, on a cold November Saturday, we headed for Berkshire Motor Works, the nearest BMW dealer, located fifty miles away in Pittsfield, Massachusetts. Mike and I figured it was a good time of year to make a deal since selling motorcycles throughout New England in November is about as brisk as selling Christmas ornaments in May. It's already too cold to ride, signaling, as it does, the beginning of a seemingly endless winter in which most motorcyclists must be content with memories of their summer rides.

There were no customers in the dealership that day, so the young owner, Ron, was in the back. In the showroom were new BMW models: a yellow-and-blue futuristic-looking K1; a dark blue K100RS sporting a powerful four-cylinder engine—an autobahn blaster; and an adventure bike, the R100GS with the traditional two opposed cylinders, an air-cooled street bike. However, Mike and I were immediately drawn to the sleek, red K75S in the center of the floor, the three-cylinder little sister to the K100. It had all the latest in BMW technology, was described as their "entry-level" bike, and was, well, beautiful.

While beauty in bikes is in the eye of the beholder, the K75S was an exceptional machine. It looked as if it had been sculpted rather than assembled. It had flowing lines, a minimum of odd parts and loose wires, and an elegant unity of purpose about it, without loud graphics or forced styling. It had a small fiberglass fairing that could route the wind around the rider but was not so large as to completely cover the engine; it functioned, as lingerie does, not to draw undue attention to itself but to enhance what is already inherently intriguing. Having experienced lust at first sight without riding the bike (which would not have been allowed since we didn't have motorcycle licenses), without even asking the shop owner to let us hear what the engine sounded like we made a cash offer to buy two of them.

A few weeks later a matched pair of red Beemers arrived by trailer at Mike's barn, where they sat unridden for the winter. Imprisoned in a New York City apartment during weekdays, I read and reread the owner's manual for my K75S; I also subscribed to every major motorcycle magazine and read every article and ad to learn as much as I could about the adventure I had begun. Each weekend, Mike and I crunched through the snow to the barn, where we lovingly inspected our acquisitions. I examined every cable and bolt, wiped imaginary dust from the fairing, and, with a mind full of anticipated pleasures, caressed its contours. Then every few weeks I would carefully coax the battery to start the frozen engine, which would fire up my imagination.

The first photographs I have of my return to motorcycling show me bundled in a down jacket, perched on the seat of the red beauty, beaming in delight, awaiting that spring day when the expertly designed and engineered machine would carry me away into a new world of experience. My weeks of waiting generated fantasies about the carefree trips I would take throughout New England and the Adirondacks during the coming summer.

Eventually, the snow began to melt, transforming the ground into deep slush and mud, but I was growing impatient. In love with the romance of riding, I wanted desperately to try the bike. I wondered what it would actually feel like to be handling five hundred pounds of German cutting-edge engineering. One day, with the ground thawed just enough to be slippery, I awkwardly rolled the Beemer from the barn. I fired it up, clinked it into first gear, and through grass, gravel, and dirt managed to fishtail across Mike's yard and down eighty yards of unpaved easement to my house in the woods. There I proudly showed my wife, Carol Ann, that I was finally a "motorcycle man," as she had already affectionately dubbed my emerging identity. Of course, I was hardly a motorcyclist at that point, more like a boy with an awkward new toy. I would have to wait a few more weeks for my first real road test, until the mud and ice on the quarter-mile easement dried enough so that I, proud owner of this K75S, could roll it to the nearest paved country road.

Finally, in early March 1991 the easement tempo-
rarily dried and, although the air temperature was in
the 30s, much too cold for an extended motorcycle
ride, it was not too cold to keep an eager man from his
maiden voyage. On a brisk Saturday morning, knowing
that Mike and I planned to go for our first ride, Carol
Ann took our picture and then went grocery shopping.
I had already purchased a black leather jacket but did
not yet possess the other equipment that the magazines
suggested for riding: leather riding pants, a full face
helmet, motorcycle gloves, and boots. So I suited up
the way I usually did in the winter when I walked in the
woods to cut firewood: long johns under jeans, layers
of shirts under a wool sweater, work boots, and work
gloves. I borrowed an old ill-fitting, open face helmet
with a flimsy shield from Mike. I was beside myself
with excitement. Mike was more subdued and confident,
reflecting his greater skill and riding experience.

At noon under a bright blue sky, bundled up like
the Pillsbury Doughboy, I carefully followed Mike
down the easement and onto the narrow country road
that meandered through rolling farm country. Having
ridden smaller motorcycles twenty years before, I was
vaguely familiar with the mechanics of shifting, accel-
erating, and braking, but the power, size, and weight
of the K75S were new to me. As we traveled, using
only first and second gear, the bike, which had been

awkward to balance in the barn, flowed along the road. The quiet purr of the engine and exhaust, the superior engineering, and the cold breeze in my face reduced my anxiety and inspired confidence.

After less than a mile, we turned onto an even narrower road and climbed carefully up a small hill. At the top we turned right and began a descent along the western slope as the road meandered through a one-hundred-year-old working farm and then through several S-turns as it cut through plowed fields exposed recently from the melted snow. I was mesmerized by the picturesque winding road, the ancient farmhouse that had sheltered generations, the rounded brown hills capped by a pristine dome of blue sky, and my new motorcycle.

I was so struck by the beauty of the setting and overwhelmed by my swelling feelings of joy that I neglected to pay attention to where I was going. To my utter horror, my tires dropped a few inches off the pavement onto a narrow strip of loose gravel that separated the pavement from a drainage ditch. I had neglected to keep my K75S on the road around a gentle left-handed downhill turn. In an instant, my ecstasy converted to panic. I knew instinctively and from studying safety tips in magazines that gravel was very dangerous, that I should not turn fast or try to brake. What to a skilled rider would have been an easily

Fateful country road, Brunswick, New York

remediable mistake was to me insurmountable. Being less than ten minutes into my return to motorcycling, I had no automatic repertoire of skills for handling this machine around a gravel turn. In that instant, I spotted what looked like a narrow dirt path built as a bridge for farm equipment between the gravel shoulder of the road and the fallow sloping field. Faced with a choice of trying to turn on gravel or ride on the dirt path, I opted for the path toward the field.

My front tire dropped over the edge, causing the bike to stop suddenly, and I became airborne, flying horizontally six feet high, then headfirst into the plowed field. Upon my return to earth, my first point of contact was the flimsy plastic face shield of the helmet, which shattered on impact. Next my tortoise-shell eyeglasses were smashed, opening a series of cuts on the bridge of my nose. Then my neck and right shoulder absorbed the brunt of the utterly graceless landing. Stunned, half blinded by dirt, blood, and lack of glasses, I lifted myself up and heard my beloved Beemer still running, lying on its right side twenty feet below me. I stumbled to the bike and hit the kill switch, at which point my fantasy world of motorcycling also died.

Standing alone in the winter silence, staring at the fractured motorcycle, I was emotionally shattered— not just from being bruised and bloodied but also from feeling humiliated and defeated. I was no master of this machine or of myself. I had allowed my emotions to impair my perceptions and permitted my fantasies of motorcycling to override awareness of my lack of skill.

A minute later Mike returned, incredulous that I could have crashed on such a gentle curve at such a careful pace. Equally thankful for and embarrassed by his presence, I allowed him to take charge. My K75S was ridable but, he knew, not by me. After finding that I was physically okay, he rode back to the barn to retrieve his car while I waited with my battered bike on the side of the empty road. It was an interminable fifteen minutes. I knew I would never have an inspiring first ride again. I could hardly stand to look at the damage to the bike or think about the wounds on my face, or confront my own stupidity. My beautiful bike would never be new again, and I would never again be so naïve about motorcycling. The vision of riding that had for months brought excitement into my life now harbored a swelling apprehension. The dangers of motorcycling had become as clear as the sky. I knew at that moment that motorcycling was going to be a much greater challenge than I had anticipated and that mastering this new sport was going to take much longer than I had expected. But I didn't yet fully appreciate that many months would pass before I would be able to get on the bike again without first conquering a mountain of fear and doubts about my ability to ever be a skilled motorcyclist.

After Mike returned with his car, I drove it home as he maneuvered my mangled motorcycle. Carol Ann had encouraged my sudden fascination with motorcycles, and now I worried about the effect my crash might have on her enthusiasm. Maybe it was the fact that Mike and I were already back in the barn when she drove past on her way home from grocery shopping, or maybe it was the telepathic connection that two people have after living together for many years, but she knew something had happened even before I made the somber walk to our house. In the end, she was understanding. The major obstacle I needed to confront was within me.

My first task was to repair the damaged fairing. As penance for my mistakes, I made myself fix the bike rather than have the BMW shop repair it, even though I am about as handy at mechanics as I am in the kitchen. While waiting for the real riding season to begin that spring, and under Mike's tutelage, I fiberglassed the broken pieces of fairing; replaced the shattered lights; and sanded, primed, and repainted the repaired pieces. But the K75S was never again pristine. My patchwork looked like patchwork. My attempt at painting looked like attempted painting. I was similarly blemished. Each morning as I shaved, the scars on my nose were evident in the mirror, and each night the scars on my psyche were reflected in nightmares of crashing. Even if others could not readily spot the imperfections on my bike or in me, they were there, always a reminder of my naïveté, always a dark warning.

However, in the long run the fear engendered by that first fateful ride proved to be good. When I resumed riding later that spring and found that the experience consisted of 95 percent anxiety and 5 percent pleasure, to master my fear I vowed to master the art of motorcycling. With the bike repaired, the weather warmer, and my confidence partially restored, I began a self-imposed schedule of training. Every weekend I spent hours slowly and cautiously practicing riding, first in empty parking lots and then on empty country roads, acquiring a learner's permit later that summer. While developing skills and overcoming fear, I struggled to be both therapist and patient, teacher and student. Previously, I had understood motorcycling only by reading articles, but now I had to master the physical skills of riding as well as the emotional and cognitive skills of managing my own anxieties and enthusiasm. Motorcycling, I discovered, required dedication and discipline, not unbridled exuberance. It became clear that my return to motorcycling was not going to be a simple ride in the country, at least not if I wanted to stay unbroken and alive.

For my next three years and thirty thousand miles of riding the K75S, there was a special bond between us. I would like to think that it eventually forgave me for my early transgression, and I know I rode it with full attention and respect as it instructed me in the subtle mysteries of motorcycling. But its most influential lesson, one I still carry with me on every ride, occurred in that second mile under the cold, blue March sky.

Track Day at Willow Spring International Raceway c. 1996

2. Terrors of the Track

WHEN PURCHASING a motorcycle in 1990, I was given a promotional gift from BMW: an offer to participate at no cost in something called CLASS, a popular training program for motorcycle riders given at various locations across the country. At first I paid no attention to it because as a teacher I felt I had already spent too much of my life in classes and, in fact, had decided to ride motorcycles to take me away from classes. But after considering that I had crashed my new K75S on my first ride I realized that I needed all the help I could get.

At the time, I was deep into self-help: I subscribed to every moto magazine, such as *Cycle World*, *Motorcyclist*, *Rider*, *Motorcycle Consumer News*, and *BMW Owners News*, devouring each article about rider safety, road hazards, protective gear, and building riding skills. At

every opportunity I took Amtrak from Manhattan up
the Hudson River to rural upstate, where my K75S was
still stored in Mike's barn, and meandered, with or
without Mike, for hours on paved country roads near
the Vermont border. I was very slowly gaining confidence, mastering the physics of riding, and learning to
cruise tentatively at 30 or 40 mph on empty stretches
of road. Apart from dropping my bike once while making a U-turn on a sloping narrow country road, I had
kept the bike upright for several months, allowing
myself to think that I might have a chance at mastering
this machine.

Eventually, the offer of a training class looked
increasingly appealing. Since it was cosponsored by the
distinguished company BMW, I assumed that the program wouldn't entice new buyers like me into anything
risky, and I needed help with my barely diminished
anxiety about riding. Since 1972 the program had
been directed by Reg Pridmore, a renowned racer and
a three-time American Motorcycle Superbike champ
and Motorcycle Hall of Fame member, who had won
a Daytona race on a BMW. It was a program geared
toward ordinary street riders, not racers, and its mission was to teach skills to a range of motorcyclists,
from those with as little as three months' experience
to riders with over forty years of experience. Since I had

been riding for almost three months, I figured I could rise to the challenge and convinced Mike to join me.

The program was being offered in a quaint village in the Finger Lakes region of central New York, a seemingly perfect confluence of scenic environment, warm weather, and opportunity to improve my riding skills and reduce my anxieties, I thought. As a clincher, Mike's brother lived there, and so we would have a free place to board the night before the training, which was a few weeks away. All I had to do was get there—not such an easy task for a novice as it was a two-hundred-mile trip each way. I had never ridden on roads other than small, relatively empty county ones, but the trip to the Finger Lakes would entail taking a New York state tollway, with high speed limits and traffic—conditions that worried me. It was as if I would now have to take off the training wheels for my first real motorcycle trip. The night before the departure my sleep was disturbed with excitement and worry yet also with hopeful anticipation.

The next morning as I transitioned from the on-ramp to Interstate 90 with its 65 mph speed limit and fast-moving traffic, I felt anxious but exhilarated. Mustering courage, I slowly twisted the throttle and eased up to 60 mph. I might have been the slowest vehicle on the interstate that day, but I was traveling way over my comfort zone and felt I was frigging flying. My anxiety lessened with each mile until we unexpectedly entered a road construction zone. As the traffic slowed, 40 mph seemed comparatively sedate until I realized that I now had to cope with uneven pavement and loose gravel, with cars and trucks behind me. To experienced motorcyclists, such construction zones are insignificant, but to me they had potential for an impending disaster, and my anxiety meter went back into the red zone, my imagination alive with images of falling down and being squished by the eighteen-wheeler behind me. Eventually, the construction zone ended and the trip continued.

After two hundred miles, I had learned to travel at 60 mph in a straight line with my anxiety modestly under control. When we arrived at Mike's brother's home, I had a deep sense of personal accomplishment. I was relieved and, though able to pretend that the trip had been no particular challenge, ready for a strong drink. I allowed myself to hope that this might be the onset of achieving my unrealized ambition: not just to ride a motorcycle but to become a skilled motorcyclist.

The next morning, we arrived at the training site, the Watkins Glen International Speedway, which was considered North America's premier and fastest racing facility. Since 1948 "The Glen" had had a storied past from its Formula 1 Grand Prix roots to its distinction as New York's only home to the NASCAR Sprint Cup Series. I felt overwhelmed. The twisting racetrack, which snaked for over two miles past grandstands and fences, was stunning in its beauty and promise but also looked intimidating. The caliber of legendary drivers who had taken the turns of Watkins Glen International was nearly second to none. Superstars from all forms of racing—open-wheel, sports car, and stock car—had come to The Glen to put their talent to the test, including Jimmy Clark, Graham Hill, Jackie Stewart, Mario Andretti, Jeff Gordon, and Derek Bell. It was as if I had been a mediocre Little League second stringer who had entered Yankee Stadium and was expected momentarily to be at the plate to bat. Terrified yet unable to see any face-saving way to back out of this unfolding drama, I decided to just do what I was told to do and pretend I was familiar with track riding.

We were advised that our motorcycles had to be inspected before we could participate in the training on the track. The tires had to be nearly new, and the bikes couldn't be leaking oil. My bike had no problem passing inspection since my K75S wasn't even broken in yet.

Then we were instructed to tape over the headlights and taillights and remove or tape the rearview mirrors, a baffling instruction since lights and mirrors are essential safety features to be used when braking, turning, and being aware of what's beside and behind. Then it dawned on me: race bikes don't have lights or mirrors, and this was a racetrack.

The dozens of men and women who had signed up for the Watkins Glen training were young and old, riding a broad array of Japanese, Italian, British, and German models, including street-legal race bikes, everyday standards, and some dual sport (off-road and on-road) bikes. There were undoubtedly a few American-made Harley-Davidsons. Most participants had, like me, ridden their bikes to the track. There was no obvious way for me to know whether they were newbies or experienced riders, but one scene is indelibly etched into my memory. A car came into the parking area towing an enclosed trailer. The car's license plate indicated that the driver was from Canada, making me think the long distance was why he had the trailer. Then he rolled out a race-track-prepped blood-red Ducati equipped with safety wire and racing tires. He clearly was not a newbie there for rider training. As it turned out, he was one of a number of experienced riders who had come to sharpen their motorcycling skills by riding the famed circuit, which otherwise was closed to amateur motorcyclists. If the sport here had been snow skiing, I was there to snowplow the bunny hill while my colleague with the Ducati was there for the black diamond slopes. Again I anguished about what I had gotten myself into.

I sought temporary solace in recalling what I had read in the advertisement for the training program—that participants would be divided into two groups, one for experienced riders, described as "multiple-time repeaters"—a term with criminal justice connotations, suggesting addicts, thieves, wife-beaters, or serial killers—and a second group for everyone else. Still, this did not provide much reassurance that I had enrolled in a safety school for beginners.

After the bike inspections were completed, participants gathered in a building, where we would be welcomed by Reg Pridmore and given an orientation to the day's training session. Safety and learning were the explicit goals. We were told that the training was to improve riding skills so we could ride faster and with more confidence. The participants could place themselves in either of the two groups. We were going to spend the day in classroom instruction interspersed with practice riding around the track to improve our skills in braking, cornering, and engine management. When we were on the track, instructors would be riding with us to show, by example, how to get around the race circuit. There was to be no passing other bikes on the right, although passing on the left was fine. Even though I was sitting in a classroom with dozens of others dressed in full protective riding gear, there was no way to know who was an expert and who was inexperienced. I was hoping I wasn't the only novice and others were just as petrified as I. I will soon find out, I told myself as we were instructed to put on our helmets and gloves and meet at the entrance to the track on our bikes.

We were advised that we were going to ride slowly as a group with the instructors for one lap of the track, stopping several times to gather together, when instructors would describe strategies for entering particular curves. This was the "sighting lap" so that we could learn about the subtleties of the track, the rising or falling elevations, the camber (slope) of the pavement, and the line we should take through each corner to set up for the subsequent corner. The procedure was similar to what skilled golfers do when playing on a course new to them: walk ahead to determine the slope of the fairway, the placement of hazards such as trees or sand traps, and the curvature of the green when putting. Golfers, however, do not have to strategize about a new fairway every two seconds.

As the riders followed the instructors from one corner to the next stop, I had trouble keeping up with what was clearly for them the very slow pace of the sighting lap. Whatever minimal confidence I had was quickly evaporating. I was growing certain that I might be much better off just sitting in the bleachers and observing for the day, that Watkins Glen was beyond my ability, and that I shouldn't have gotten myself into this potential debacle. My head spinning, I contemplated a furtive exit.

I was not fearing for my life, expecting to crash or get hurt. I wasn't too concerned about what others thought, although I was self-conscious about my lack of motorcycling skills. It wasn't the potential for hurt or humiliation that was making me want to flee. It was the shattering realization that my lofty goal of being a competent motorcyclist was far beyond the horizon and that the only way of possibly achieving it was to conquer my doubts. However, I also realized that to conquer my doubts I needed to complete the training program.

After another classroom session, we were to select the group of riders we should be in, which was a no-brainer for me. I only wished there had been a third group, one for the freaked-out second-string Little Leaguers who wanted to practice in the school yard rather than Yankee Stadium.

When it was my group's turn to take to the track for twenty minutes, I followed the other riders out there. At this point we were to go at our own speed and become familiar with the feel of the racetrack and its dozen turns. But instead of riding in a group we quickly became dispersed around the track as the faster riders pulled ahead. The best of this "slower" group were quite experienced riders, not race caliber but able to stay ahead of the rest on the straightaways and through the various corners, in a fashion I could only dream of doing. But since I quickly fell behind I could ride at my own comfort level, which was so slow that the fastest riders in the group started lapping me almost immediately. Everyone lapped me—the experienced, the novices, and the women. As they whizzed by me in a ballet of motion, I saw for the first time in my life what handling a five-hundred-pound motorcycle competently looked like. Suddenly, rather than feeling humiliated as they passed me I was inspired by what mere mortals could do with motorcycles. Thus while I rode psychologically alone on the track, I was continually being passed by dozens of leather-clad riders who were unwittingly encouraging me.

Back in the classroom, after one of the early track sessions, Pridmore asked the group how many of them had been going over 100 mph on the back straight, and a majority raised their hands. Having only gotten up the courage to go 60 mph, I was the slowest rider at Watkins Glen that day, maybe ever. Still, I reassured myself that I was at The Glen, riding the world-famous track and pretending to be a motorcyclist. And, much to my delight, I was beginning to enjoy it immensely.

My enjoyment was supported by the important advantages that riding on a track has over riding on the street. It isn't only that there are no speed limits or police, but because it is possible to ride the same lap over and over, the same corners and straights, the track gradually becomes as familiar as a favorite pair of shoes. In riding the same lap repeatedly, you find the best entry line into each corner and you learn the precise speed you need, when to brake, and how quickly to accelerate through the bend. The constant repetition helps you discover what is safely possible for you and builds confidence. As your fears lessen, you relax more and manage your motorcycle with increased competence. All this is enhanced by the absence of common street hazards: no sand or gravel to cause a slide or crash while the rider is leaned over in a corner; no intersections or cross traffic, which in street riding are major causes of accidents as car drivers pull out in front of riders; and no deer springing from the brush. In essence, tracks represent contrived environments that allow you to become a better street rider.

In the course of that day at The Glen, as we shuttled between the classroom and track, my anxieties subsided. I learned about throttle management, cornering, and the incredible ability of motorcycles to lean over safely in the corners at very rapid speeds. Although such maneuvers were not characteristic of my laps that day, I watched others roar past me as they dived into corners at speeds that seemed suicidal but weren't even

reckless, with these riders merely displaying motorcycling competence. Although their feats appeared
extraordinary to me at first, by the end of the day I had
seen what motorcycling could be like. With a willingness
to learn, a dedication to persistent practice, and abid-
ing patience with my own hesitancy and limitations, I
believed I might eventually achieve a similar level of
competence.

As we were dismissed at the end of the day, I was
grateful that my initial terror had been transformed
into a sense of modest accomplishment. My motorcycling skills were still very rudimentary, but I had
improved. I was undoubtedly still the slowest rider
as we left The Glen, but the more important insight
for me was that measuring myself against the skills of
others was irrelevant. The real measure was whether
I was becoming a better rider. Anticipating my two-
hundred-mile trip back home on the interstate, I felt
no panic. As I cruised along, I noted how much more
at ease I felt than I had two days before. I was alert
and cautious, to be sure, but I traveled with more confidence, kept my anxiety under control, and started to
more freely enjoy the ride. I had survived the terrors of
the track, and I allowed myself to think that I might be
able to become a motorcyclist someday.

In the years that followed, I would participate in
other track days, including a CLASS with Reg Pridmore

at Willow Springs, California, nearly three thousand miles from Watkins Glen. But the program at Watkins Glen would always represent the very beginning of my advancement as a rider. As far as I was concerned, I was the rookie who had knocked the ball out of the park that day.

The Rock Store on any Sunday

3. Finding My Niche

SOME MOTORCYCLISTS PREFER to ride solo, and others do not; each mode has advantages. Motorcycling is, in a fundamental and vital sense, a solo activity. Even with a passenger on board, only the rider has an unobstructed view; chooses the direction of travel; and manages the balance, brakes, throttle, clutch, and transmission. Unlike in sports such as baseball, soccer, or volleyball, a rider does not require the presence of others, such as a passenger or an accompanying solo rider, to fully enjoy the experience of motorcycling. Whether on metropolitan streets, county roads, or major highways across the great empty expanse of much of North America, people riding alone on motorcycles is a common sight. This solitary experience, which for many is one of the pleasures of motorcycling, entails the simple satisfaction of being in motion and not having to engage in conversation or listen to others jabbering. Especially for those with overcrowded and stressed lives, being alone and unreachable is a savored indulgence, an opportunity for contemplation, autonomy, and observation.

The advantages to riding with other motorcyclists are equally significant. First, perhaps, is the reassurance that if something should go wrong you have a companion to help you or get assistance. Also, good companionship heightens many travel experiences.

When I started motorcycling, I often rode alone. I had little choice. I knew no one who rode a motorcycle except Mike, who was often unavailable to ride on days when I traveled to Upstate New York to retrieve my K75S. And after our first few brief rides together, while I was still a neophyte, I was on my own. On these initial rides, I was so absorbed in learning elementary riding skills and avoiding another mishap that I concentrated on managing a five-hundred-pound machine and failed to experience the joys of solitude. Those pleasures, however, grew as the months passed and I began riding longer distances, into Vermont and New Hampshire. Still, the three-hour Amtrak commute from New York City to pick up my motorcycle remained an obstacle to riding as much as I desired, so I began scheming about relocating my bike closer to my neighborhood. For an apartment dweller like myself, parking space was an extremely rare and prohibitively expensive luxury. However, one of my university colleagues, Edward, had recently acquired a rural B&B with a barn near the small town of New Hope, Pennsylvania, only about an hour's drive from New York, and generously offered to keep my BMW there. For about a year, this arrangement allowed me to continue riding on weekends, meandering around rural New Jersey and Pennsylvania. Eventually, as my interest in motorcycling morphed into an obsession, I pursued other storage possibilities. Several years earlier I had placed my name on the Columbia University's waiting list for a subsidized parking space in an underground garage at 125th Street, on the northern border of the Upper West Side, near the George Washington Bridge, which linked Manhattan to New Jersey. When a parking slot became available, I grabbed it so I could finally keep my K75S near my apartment and conveniently ride out of the city.

Riding out of the city was, indeed, what I did at every opportunity. When weather permitted, I was on the empty city streets early in the morning, decked out in black leather pants, jacket, and motorcycle boots, hailing a taxi to go to my parking garage. And then, within minutes, I was motorcycling either across the George Washington Bridge or north on the Taconic Parkway, away from the city and into the countryside.

Very soon my romance with riding blossomed and I began to transition from riding for training to riding for enjoyment. Motorcycling became a way to escape the routines of academia by exploring new psychological and geographic territory. My tankbag stuffed with roadmaps, I crisscrossed Connecticut and the Hudson Valley, pursuing the "blue highways," as the travel writer William Least Heat Moon labeled secondary roads. As I gained confidence, I'd bundle a bag of clothes on the bike and make more distant solo forays— to the Maine coast, for example, the famed Blue Ridge Parkway in Virginia, or Tennessee to visit a friend. I came to appreciate the motorcyclist's mantra that it is not the destination but the ride that is paramount.

Occasionally, I also began to ride with other motorcyclists and appreciate the advantages of this mode of travel. Once, Mike and I rode to New Hampshire to watch the annual motorcycle races at Loudon, where I witnessed the stunning skills of professional racers— an event that served as a stark reminder of my very modest riding skills.

At one point, when I serendipitously mentioned to a university colleague that I was now riding a motorcycle he informed me that our mutual colleague, Rob, had once ridden motorcycles. I quickly sought him out, only to learn that Rob, like many former riders, was in the closet. Sitting in our Columbia University offices, wearing our academic suits and ties, surrounded by shelves of books and the normal disarray of papers, we chatted enthusiastically about the motorcycling days of his youth. I learned that Rob had a much more impressive motorcycling past than my own two years on small bikes while in college. In his twenties, he had purchased a new Triumph, picking it up at the shipyard in New Jersey and riding it to Seattle then home to Wisconsin. Now in his forties, he had a restless glimmer in his eye as I talked enthusiastically about my immersion in motorcycling. He wanted to see my bike, which was in the barn in Pennsylvania. Arrangements were made, and Rob briefly rode it around a parking lot, becoming hooked again. When I mentioned that my friend in Upstate New York might want to sell his K75S, days later Rob owned it. Now the twin red Beemers that had once been parked in Mike's barn resided together again, this time in my parking space in New York City. By enticing another former rider to reenlist, I had spawned a new riding buddy. Because Rob had more previous riding experience than I, his reintroduction to riding caused much less anxiety, as his prior level of skills came back to him quickly—much faster, in fact, than his ability to pass the New York motorcycle licensing exam.

While our schedules were not always in sync, Rob and I made what became some of my initial extended motorcycle trips—the first in November 1992 across central Pennsylvania for several days. With temperatures in the 30s, no heated grips or electric jackets, and only minimum cold weather gear, we suffered for many miles, stopping frequently at cafés to thaw our hands and feet. During this trip, I learned the hard way about the wind chill factor in motorcycling, and I rarely rode again in the winter without proper gear.

A much more enjoyable excursion was a big loop we made the next summer to Montreal, Canada, traveling north through the Adirondacks and returning south through Vermont. As with all collaborative activities, the route, briskness of pace, and frequency of stops to stretch, eat, take pictures, and urinate needed to be worked out, with compromises made—negotiations that are unnecessary when riding solo. With two riders, these plans are usually quickly decided and unproblematic; if not, the riders are unlikely to make trips together. However, with a larger group of riders, such decision making begins to resemble academic committee meetings in which everyone has a say, much time is wasted, and strains appear.

Yet on long trips especially, riding with others can add safety, depth, and fun to an excursion. For example, many of my motorcycles were so heavy that if I dropped them while stopping at the side of an isolated road I couldn't pick them up without assistance. Then, too, several of my riding companions, having more mechanic knowledge and skill than I did, helped me diagnose and repair random glitches, which can occur with any complicated machine. A companion with a GPS can be a savior when you are disoriented and lost. Moreover, when a magnificent vista appears as you crest a mountain pass, you can stop and savor it with companions. I have shared many stunning scenes with friends while riding the Blue Ridge Parkway, the Big Sur Highway on the California coast, the Grand Staircase of southern Utah, and the Beartooth Pass to the Chief Joseph Highway on the Wyoming/ Montana border; or while encountering a thrilling stretch of S-curves through a deep canyon as I picked up the pace to enhance the adrenalin rush; or when stopping to eat and discovering an unexpected culinary delight at some out-of-the-way eatery, such as the Diablo Café in Torrey, Utah. Of course, when riding alone you can stop amidst majestic scenery and try to capture it with a cell phone camera to share with others when you return home, but it's like offering them luke-warm, stale coffee. Also, at the end of a long day with friends, after finding a place to rest for the night there is the reward of camaraderie in a local café over a drink or two and a hearty dinner to celebrate the day's ride.

When my self-identity began to emerge as a motor-cyclist, I faced the difficult challenge of taking the next step in my involvement with motorcycling—finding a network of riding companions. There are many ways to do this. Lifelong riders who stay in the same community usually establish a network of riding companions early on and ride with them over many years. Some individuals may have become motorcyclists because their friends ride and encouraged them to learn to ride as well. Others may take up riding with friends who are also learning to ride. In my case, I resumed riding after two decades of not knowing a single avid motorcyclist. As my renewed interest in riding surfaced, I encouraged my friends Mike and Rob to resume their motorcycling, and so they became my first riding companions while I lived in New York.

Soon thereafter, however, I received an unexpected job offer in Los Angeles and decided to return to the state where I had grown up and where my extended family still resided. At the time, I did not know a single motorcyclist in California, but I was keenly aware from the motorcycling magazines that Southern California had robust motorcycling communities. The task would now be to find riding companions by locating the right motorcyclist hangouts.

I knew that discovering the right motorcyclist hangouts was key to finding not only riding companions but also my niche in a motorcycling community. I had already undertaken such a quest on the East Coast.

There a fellow rider had advised me that a café called Marcus Dairy, about seventy miles north of New York City, was the best-known motorcycle hangout in the Northeast on Sunday mornings and a likely place to meet other riders. The café, in the early 1900s, was a small family dairy in rural Connecticut owned by the Marcus family, who sold their cows in the 1940s and then established the Dairy Bar Restaurant in 1947 in Danbury that served ice cream and food, eventually becoming known as Marcus Dairy. It was located at the intersection of two highways near many roads that branched out into the New England countryside.

Following the tipster's advice, one Sunday I rode to the café, where I soon discovered that I was by no means alone with my moto obsession. I had begun motorcycling largely on my own and had coped single-handedly with my intense interest in riding, occasionally wondering what strange psychological disorder must be causing my fascination with an activity thought by others to be bizarre and dangerous. On any Sunday (the title of a famous film documentary about motorcycling) in the parking lot at Marcus Dairy, hundreds of people, from business titans to busboys of all ages and ethnicities, gathered peaceably to share opinions, experiences, and aspirations related to their insuppressible passion for motorcycles. The motorcycles they rode were as eclectic as the people themselves—there were Japanese, German, Italian, British, and American brands of all sizes and vintages. Some of the riders had ridden all their lives, and others, like me, were novices. It was a moto community from which I could gain support and inspiration.

Aware that most large metropolitan areas have hangouts like Marcus Dairy, where motorcyclists gather on weekends, and eager to find my niche upon arriving in Los Angeles with my wife, I asked Ann Berger, the owner of Marty's, a small BMW dealership, where the local motorcyclist hangouts were. I learned that in the LA area the better-known hangouts were the Rock Store, in the hills above the Malibu coast, and Newcomb's Ranch, a café in the San Gabriel Mountains above Pasadena. Northern California had Alice's Restaurant nestled in the scenic hills above Silicon Valley and the Bovine Bakery in the quaint coastal enclave of Point Reyes Station. All these destinations were accessible only by traversing twisty country roads through the hills, making them problematic for urban drivers but a siren's call for motorcyclists.

Soon I went in search of Newcomb's Ranch. To reach the café I took the 210 Freeway to La Canada Flintridge, then headed north on Highway 2 as it climbed up about five thousand feet into the mountains above Los Angeles, following the road for about thirty miles. The route, known as the Angeles Crest

Highway, is a stunning snake of a two-lane road that continues for sixty miles of unending curves through forests, along cliff-hanging tarmac littered with fallen rocks from the steep slopes, and ends in the small hamlet of Wrightwood. Because of the elevation and freezing temperatures, much of the highway is closed to traffic in the winter.

On my first ascent up the "Crest," I traveled as swiftly as my skills permitted, about the speed of the average car driver. It was a stimulating road that demanded attention. But I soon realized that my focus was riveted on my rearview mirrors, where I could see motorcyclists gaining rapidly on me and then whizzing by at speeds I hadn't seen in New England. Anxieties about my riding skills, absent for many months, quickly surfaced again. In awe, I realized this was a Sunday morning racetrack and I was an imposter! While I was duly impressed with their grace, control, and speed, I felt as I had at Watkins Glen three years before, wondering what was I doing there, thinking I was a dachshund in a land of greyhounds, and concluding in short order that California riding was different.

After being passed by swarms of motorcyclists for thirty miles, I arrived at the rustic Newcomb's Ranch café. The parking lot was filled with hundreds of bikes and many riders decked out in colorful full leathers. More so than at Marcus Dairy, this was a playground for those who rode race-replica bikes—Ducatis and 1000cc Japanese sport bikes—and rode them well. While the mix of folks was also eclectic, many were the slalom skiers of motorcycling: those with advanced skills, sleek powerful machines, and a willingness to push to the raggedy edge of sanity, for fun. It was easy to imagine going wide on a decreasing-radius turn over a cliff or into a guardrail or tree; indeed, I later learned there was a disturbing annual casualty rate on the Angeles Crest Highway on weekends. Over the years that followed, I continued to ride that highway periodically, becoming, in time, a middling greyhound, passing as many bikes as passed me. But on that first ride Newcomb's Ranch didn't seem to be my niche so I continued looking for the right hangout.

I next went in search of the Rock Store on the Mulholland Highway above Malibu. In the early twentieth century the Rock Store had been a stagecoach stop nestled within the hills between the San Fernando Valley and Pacific Coast. In 1961, Ed and Vern (Veronica) Salvo purchased the building and converted it into a small-town grocery store and then a café open only on weekends. Over the years it became one of the most famous motorcycle destinations in the country, well-known among riders from around the world, and it also became a common site for movie, television, and magazine shoots. Subscribers to motorcycle magazines have seen many photos taken in this area. Among the hundreds of riders who frequent the hangout are devotees of vintage bikes, racing-endowed sport bikes, chrome-encrusted Harleys, one-of-a-kind specially designed motorcycles, and the entire array of street, sport-touring, and dirt bikes. A large measure of its fame, however, is its location among canyons providing a network of scenic, narrow, twisty roads that are just short of a nightmare for car drivers but constitute a wet dream for sport bike riders. None of this history was known to me when I rode up the Mulholland Highway for the first time, nor could I have sensed that the Rock Store would become the center of my riding life every Saturday and Sunday morning for the next ten years.

The general routine at the Rock Store was to use the site as a place to meet riding companions, perhaps have a coffee, breakfast, or lunch, and go riding. The reward was not the quality of the coffee or food; it was the abundance and quality of the surrounding roads. The dozens of roads offer a potpourri of experience, from the fast sweepers of Encinal to the torturous, narrow, hairpin turns of Stunt Road as it drops precipitously to the ocean. Almost all these roads, carved through the rocky dry hills, offer glimpses of the Pacific Ocean and vistas that can mesmerize riders into dangerous inattention if they are not vigilant.

I had found the territory that would serve as my training ground and advance my riding skills. Now I needed to find my niche within this diverse community. I began riding to the Rock Store early every Saturday and Sunday morning, fourteen miles on twisty roads from our house in Corral Canyon in the Santa Monica Mountains. Josephina, who greeted the flow of riders entering the café, would pour me a cup of joe, after which I would stroll around the parking lot admiring the constantly changing display of bikes and chatting with other leather-clad riders.

One of the advantages of having a shared obsession is that it brings diverse people together. On about my second or third weekend at the Rock Store, I talked with the rider of a BMW K100RS, Ryan, a decade-long Rock Store regular, who invited me to join him for breakfast. While sitting at one of the couple dozen tables inside, we talked not just about bikes but also about ourselves. He was the owner of a successful business who, like me, had become a motorcyclist in mid-life, although otherwise our lives didn't overlap in many ways. Ryan began graciously introducing me to a web of other Rock Store regulars—some lifelong riders, others midlife converts, some cautious riders, others former racers. It turned out that Ryan knew only one other person at UCLA, where I now taught, and that was because the fellow, David, was also a Rock

Store regular. I eventually befriended this other academic and rode with him for many years. Curiously, although his office at the university was only a hundred yards from mine, we saw each other only when dressed in leathers.

In general, the Rock Store regulars were a heterogeneous, perhaps motley, group bound together primarily by their attachment to motorcycling. There were single guys in their twenties and grandfathers; the unemployed, the retired, and the working-overwhelmed; as well as a few whose occupations remained deliberately vague. I got to know several dozen with whom I rode routinely on weekend mornings and came to view as friends. There were many others whom I knew by face and motorcycle but not by name. Nevertheless, when encountering one another we could casually continue any fragmented conversation about bikes that we had begun a few weeks or months earlier, with the ease of old friends. Ryan's willingness to share breakfast with me, a newcomer in LA and at the Rock Store, was the big break I had needed to find my place in the local community of motorcycle riders. And within a year I had become, for the first time, a regular member of a group of motorcyclists.

Along with finding one's niche in a motorcycling community comes the discovery that there are often pronounced differences among avid motorcyclists.

Though they share a love of motorcycling, they can be classified by loyalty to certain brands or types of motorcycling, much like sports fans may love baseball or football. Of the motorcyclists who are loyal to brands, the largest group consists of those who like Harley-Davidsons, the big, heavy cruisers. Although they suffer from the stereotype of being roughneck louts, they are, in fact, a diverse group composed only partially of some real hooligans while others only pretend to be. Other motorcyclists are loyal to motos made in Britain (Triumph, Norton), Italy (Ducati, Moto Guzzi, Aprilia), Germany (BMW), and Japan (Honda, Suzuki, Yamaha, and Kawasaki) as well as to motorcycle manufacturers in Austria and elsewhere. They can also have a loyalty to antique/vintage bikes in general.

Additionally, motorcyclists can be classified by their riding preferences: cruising, sport, sport-touring, dirt, dual sport, or adventure riding. Manufacturers know these preferences and make a variety of models that cater to different riding inclinations. For example, Suzuki makes race-replica sport bikes but also big Harleyesque cruisers. Yamaha makes fine small dirt bikes and long-distance touring rigs. BMW makes racing bikes and big adventure models. Moreover, many riders, like me, have multiple identities. For example, my garage usually houses several bikes, and at times

An evolving collection

I've owned simultaneously a sport, a sport-touring, and a dirt bike, all made by different manufacturers.

Many motorcyclists have preferences that are not obvious to nonriders but instantaneously recognizable to most motorcyclists simply by the apparel of the rider or even the distinct sounds of an engine. Most motorcyclists can distinguish by sound a single-cylinder from a two-cylinder engine, a Ducati V-twin from a Harley V-twin engine, a boxer engine from an in-line four-cylinder Japanese bike, and so on. That is why when two motorcyclists meet each other for the first time an early inquiry will be: "What bikes do you have?" The answers will situate them in the universe of motorcycling, in terms of brands, models, and type of riding, just as having a fly rod locates a fisherman in the fishing universe.

Within a year I had become a regular at the Rock Store, and hanging around there with the motorcyclists had helped me recognize my location in this universe, which had begun with sport-touring. During the first year, I traded the K75S for a new BMW R1100RS as soon as that new model debuted in 1994. While the RS would be my primary motorcycle for the next five years, it soon was not my only ride. The Rock Store credo, I learned, was if having one bike was good owning more was better. Since then I have never had only one bike, and at one point I had as many as five. I first added a Ducati 900SS, replaced by a Honda VFR or two, then briefly an RC51 as I migrated over a few years toward sport bikes. Then I started swapping bikes for larger and more comfortable sport-touring bikes, such as Honda's 1300ST, the BMW K1200RS, and a string of Moto Guzzis. Beemers have been my mainstay since 1991, and I don't recall ever being without at least one in my garage. Over the years, I've owned about thirty bikes, but in recent years I have returned to my roots in sport-touring, with a little off-road dual-sport riding for diversion.

The variety of riders who flooded into the Rock Store parking lot changed as each weekend day progressed. Early in the day you'd find the Beemer guys; later in the morning it would be the hard-core sport riders as the younger guys recovering from partying the night before headed into the canyons with testosterone-fueled enthusiasm. By afternoon, it was predominately a middle-aged and older Harley group with polished chromed bikes, eating and drinking under the California oak trees, content and in no hurry to go anywhere else. For many of the Beemer guys, the Rock Store was a place to plan a day's ride; for the sport bikers, a place to pause and check out the display of race-replica machinery; for the Harley crowd, it appeared to be the destination.

Among the hundreds of riders hustling into and out of the Rock Store each weekend, I was usually part of the first wave, the early morning riders, who tended to be either the older guys who didn't sleep well, arose early, and had short or nonexistent "honey do" lists and relatively few pressing familial obligations or those who sought to escape from the weekday stresses of work and find low-stress camaraderie and the thrill of riding. We would begin arriving about 7:00 am, be fortified with coffee by 8:00 am, and, having planned the day's ride with a few buddies, launch into the canyons by 9:00 am or so. The Rock Store provided many destinations beyond the Santa Monica Mountains— the Crest, Ojai, Los Olivos, and Bodfish/Caliente. Each entailed an intriguing ride that avoided, as much as possible, the clogged major highways, maximizing the miles traveled on empty twisty roads. In our motor-cycling logic, the best route from A to B was not the shortest or fastest but the longest and most twisty.

At any time of day, the diverse group at the Rock Store had a casual disregard for others' personal fortunes, marital histories, parenting styles, and religious or political orientations. It only mattered that motor-cycling was a central part of your life and that you could talk intently about the comparative advantages of tires or brake pads, the aesthetics of the latest Ducati, or the implications of the new BMW engine design.

I learned during my early years at the Rock Store that, after becoming absorbed in the culture of motor-cycling, there are always topics you can easily and safely talk about with other motorcyclists, as is common among any two strangers who discover they are both architects, social workers, photographers, barbers, or triathletes, and thus share important personal observations and concerns. While engaged in such conversations, I realized that my striving to acquire the skills to be a competent motorcyclist and find my niche among a community of riders had given way to recognition that I had become one of this marvel-ously ragtag collective of riders for whom being on two wheels constituted who they naturally were. This identity wasn't bestowed by others, earned through a managed sequence of tests, or attained through completion of an initiatory event; rather, it emerged internally. I started to notice, for example, that when strangers asked me what I did or who I was, I was as likely to reply "motorcyclist" as I was "professor" or "father."

Over ten years of being a Rock Store regular, I had bonded closely with the small group of guys I rode with every weekend. We were often joined by others from a familiar network of several dozen early rising, seriously obsessed motorcyclists. All were experienced riders though some more skilled, some faster, some more cautious, some saner. Riding with this group became a collective ballet that required familiarity and trust.

Our gatherings at the Rock Store focused on motorcycles and motorcycling, not on our personal histories. Although in time, over dozens of day rides together, multiple-day excursions to the mountains, and trips to the races at Laguna Seca, we did learn about each other's ambitions, sorrows, and life experiences. I often marveled at how groups of men differed from groups of women when it came to focusing on personal matters. When women riders met each other for the first time, if given even fifteen minutes to chat they were likely to know whether they were or had been married, had children, where they grew up, and what they did for a living. In similar circumstances, men sometimes did not know each other's names, although they would remember exactly what model of bike they rode and what accessories had been added. What women riders knew in fifteen minutes would take male motorcyclists, including myself, about fifteen months to discover. Eventually, my regular riding partners began getting together socially with their spouses, some of whom would ride two-up with them. I can remember seeing my buddies for the first time wearing shoes and slacks rather than boots and leathers. At that point, my two worlds of experience— secular and motorcycle—were beginning to blend.

Spending over a decade at the Rock Store allowed me to become part of an identity group. As motorcyclists, we were bonded by an attachment to a peculiar life regardless of our different pathways, just as those who play on a hockey team or remain in the same foursome for decades on the golf links. Perhaps the bond was meaningful to me because it was based on a core part of my identity that gave me vitality, unlike my associations with colleagues on campus with whom even after years of knowing them I might share nothing more than working in the same building. This group had no name, no membership list, no officers, no requirements for inclusion, no leaders, no differential statuses, and no length of commitment. It was a network of equals who, if asked, might disagree about who was in the group or even whether there *was* a group since members were constantly evolving as people found the Rock Store and then later disappeared. Nevertheless, the group had many shared tales about people and events, some dating back long before I appeared. Their tales, often entertainingly embellished, were about trips to Big Sur, Mendocino, Death Valley, and the Sierra Nevada Mountains; yarns of speeding tickets avoided and properly earned; laments about near misses and crashes; sagas of flat tires and broken-down motorcycles far from home; accounts of traveling in dire conditions, such as high winds across the desert, downpours on the coast, and snow and ice in the mountains.

Some of the epic stories were given titles that alone would evoke memories of the associated events. For example, when six or seven of us intrepid weekend riders encountered unexpected ice on a familiar road and instead of turning around, which might have been interpreted as lacking machismo, soldiered on, Jim labeled us "The Donner Party," a name that henceforth conjured recollections of our flawed judgment, multiple spills, and Neil's Honda 1100ST (which I had once

Northern California coast

owned) abandoned in the snow on Breckenridge Road. Such memories were part of the group's culture, meaningful milestones in our lives as motorcyclists as well as in the group's history.

As with all groups, the participants included many distinctive characters whose idiosyncrasies were only recognized after much time spent together. For example, one legendary character in our group, who had been a fixture at the Rock Store longer than just about anybody else, was Harry, a retired movie industry helicopter pilot and lifelong motorcyclist. He was notable not just for being a good, easygoing fellow but because he was always going on motorcycles. Nearly a generation older than most of the senior riders, he and his Beemer GS were permanent fixtures in the parking lot, and when he didn't appear it was noted. "Where's Harry?" we would ask each other. The answer once was that he was riding to Ohio that week to attend his sixtieth high school reunion. During another absence we learned that he had made a trip to Montana but had spontaneously decided to add a side trip to Alaska. In his seventies and eighties while making these trips alone, he had traveled over one million miles by motorcycle, many of them after his retirement. He was a symbol of hope that perhaps we, too, had years of riding left. Recently, at eighty-seven, Harry collapsed and died while riding. As one friend noted, he left us as he wanted to—in the saddle with his boots on.

But being part of this group exposed me to more than embellished tales of rides and roads. It introduced me to lives beyond my carefully sheltered professional enclave and to the tribulations of others. Some members of my adopted weekend family got married or divorced. Others changed careers or lost their jobs. Still others experienced grave diseases and recovered, while others died. I made visits to hospitals when buddies crashed, and I attended funerals. One morning following a rider's cremation, a friend came to the Rock Store and asked if anyone would help the deceased's wife scatter his ashes that day on a nearby ridge overlooking the ocean. I participated, having contemplated the same distribution for myself when my time came.

Although I have not regularly frequented the Rock Store for some years, and have had only occasional contact with individuals in my riding group, I know that when I roll in next time I will be welcomed back and our conversations will resume without missing a beat. This will occur because from about 1993 to 2004, when my weekend haunt was the Rock Store, I became not just a motorcyclist but a participant in a group of like-minded devotees.

Finding a weekend hangout and some riding compatriots provided me with a social niche in my new world of motorcycling. Instead of being a solo rider, I had become a member of a community in which many, if not most, of the others were as obsessed with motorcycles as I was. The benefits were profound. I made good friends that I've now had for decades. It encouraged me to ride more. It provided a rapid introduction to the geography of Southern California. I had great fun every weekend, which added a new dimension to my life. And perhaps most importantly, it advanced my riding skills. Finding my niche helped me make the transition from riding as training to riding as a way of life.

PART TWO

GAINING TRACTION

Crossing the Carrizo Plain, central coastal California

4. Splendid Isolation
Transformation through Riding Gear

AS I MOVED SLOWLY from novice to experienced rider, my understanding of the challenges and paradoxes of motorcycling matured, as did my awareness of its temptations and dangers. I soon learned that one of the paradoxes of motorcycling involved the effect of riding gear. Although riding gear is integral to motorcycling, I had to gradually learn that with each piece of gear I put on I incrementally left my familiar world and entered a new environment. Paradoxically, the riding gear that appeared initially to inhibit my movement and mute my senses ultimately opened up a new world of movement and vivid sensation.

Aware of the importance of riding gear after my reinvolvement with motorcycling in the late winter of 1991, having planted my face in a field wearing Mike's old open face helmet, I returned to the BMW motorcycle shop in Pittsfield, Massachusetts, accompanied by Carol Ann, to check out helmets. Since I was resuming motor- cycling after a twenty-year sabbatical, I knew it was necessary to acquire the proper gear before the riding season began. In my youth, when traveling to campus on my Yamaha 80 I basically wore only jeans, a cloth jacket, or shirt, and street shoes. However, on this return to riding, I promised my wife I would always wear protective gear.

I had been reading that helmets were the single most important piece of protection one could buy. The last time I had worn a helmet was while playing high school football, when, as quarterback and captain, I led the team on a record-shattering losing streak. A modern full face helmet was quite different, as I dis- covered in the BMW shop. I removed my glasses and tried pulling a Shoei helmet straight down over the top of my balding head, anticipating that it would never fit through the small opening—and, indeed, it was like squeezing my head into a pipe. Once the helmet was on, my whole body felt unnaturally and severely confined, as if I were preparing for a deep sea dive, missing only the weights around the waist and the lead boots. Without my glasses, I stared blurry- eyed through the transparent face shield like a diver peering through an ancient iron helmet into the murky depths. Suddenly sensing a shortage of oxygen,

I felt I might suffocate and gasped for air. My heart raced. I broke into a cold sweat, the kind that precedes fainting. My lifelong claustrophobia, usually harmless as long as I stayed out of submarines, caves, and caskets, overwhelmed me. This onset of a panic attack was only partially subdued by my fear of completely embarrassing myself in front of the shop's owner and by the comedic field day Carol Ann would have telling our friends about how her wannabe motorcyclist partner had fainted while trying on a helmet.

At that moment I couldn't imagine ever voluntarily wearing such an instrument of torture, even for a few minutes. I wanted to get the helmet off fast, but not having mastered the subtle technique for removing this device of torture, I had to beg calmly for help from the shop owner. After taking a few minutes to restore my composure, in a feeble attempt not to appear as a complete wimp I ordered a helmet, figuring I'd get used to it—with psychiatric help. As it turned out, I didn't need Prozac. Eventually I learned that the sensation of pulling on a helmet is part of a necessary physical, mental, and emotional transformation that occurs when I get ready to ride and that results in a splendid isolation allowing for intensified sensual experiences.

The immediate and obvious significance of riding gear is its enhancement of safety. Serious motorcyclists would no more refrain from wearing their riding gear than a rock climber would avoid using lines and anchors. Maybe it could be done, but why incur the additional risks? And, as other sports enthusiasts who wear special gear know, the ritual of donning such gear can mentally prepare you for participation and alter your perspective on your role.

The ritual of dressing for biking takes only a few minutes yet quickly alters not only my body but also my orientation. Although you can now buy leather gear that is as colorful as a clown's suit, my heavy leather pants are no fashion statement. They are the traditional, unimaginative black and have padding in the knees and hips. The pants are longer than my regular jeans because they are designed for sitting in the crouched position.

My tall riding boots are utilitarian; they would never pass for designer footwear. The legs of the boots, which zip up the back of my calves, fit tight and are tilted forward a few degrees to accommodate my bent legs while riding. There is extra leather on the ankles and toes for protection. They are heavy, awkward, and would be uncomfortable if I had to walk in them for any distance.

My black leather jacket, properly speckled by unlucky insects, has many features to minimize risk. It is no loose-fitting Armani knockoff that could be confused with the thin, supple haute-couture leather coats with meaningless faux zippers sold at

Bloomingdales. Rather, it is a rider's jacket, thick and snug-fitting so that it doesn't flap. The arms are made longer than normal and rotated a few degrees forward at the shoulder to fit well when I am leaning to the handlebars. It has a short, mandarin-style collar that won't slap me silly in the wind. The zippers, snaps, and Velcro fasteners allow me to securely close the front of the jacket and sleeves so that, depending on the season, frigid air or bees will not break my concentration. They also secure me in a protective shell against threats from the pavement. Special zippered vents in the front and back allow me to regulate airflow and, therefore, temperature. A wide beltlike internal structure holds and protects my kidneys and lower back. Pads on the shoulders and elbows provide added protection. Leather motorcycle jackets never go out of style and rarely wear out, accounting for why so many riders have more than one in their closet. I still wear the first two leather jackets I bought, but they are now joined in my closet by several waterproof textile varieties.

My riding leathers put me in an anticipatory frame of mind. The snug fit prepares me for the high-speed winds I am likely to encounter, while the thickness of the leather and all the protective pads remind me of the potential risks I am about to assume.

Once ensconced in my protective gear, I am encased from head to foot, unable to feel the ordinary sensations people have of going outdoors, such as the warmth of the sun. To some extent, it feels like I have dressed to go outside in winter in Wisconsin, girding the loins to enter a hostile environment. The transition then continues as I take foam earplugs from their case, roll them between my forefinger and thumb until they are elongated and push one into each ear canal to diminish normal sounds. Earplugs are not designed to protect the rider from the sound of the motorcycle itself, which is minimal and pleasant, but to block the roar of the air as it is split by a helmet. The first time I used earplugs, it was disorienting and unnerving. I sensed a palpable and unwanted loss and an immediate physical vulnerability in not being able to hear what might be happening around me—a whisper, a footstep, a door opening. Earplugs separate me from the world of subtle sounds, as occurs more profoundly for a person who is becoming deaf. To this day, the loss of familiar sounds remains momentarily unsettling. But while blocking sounds earplugs also intensify what you feel. With them in my ears, I can more readily feel the pleasant rumble of my bike, detect the click of the shifting gears and tires groaning when pushed to the limits of traction. Earplugs block distractions, allowing me to hear only those sounds that are essential for riding, and, more importantly, open new possibilities of sensing the environment.

Pulling on my helmet almost completes the transition to an environment apart from the everyday world. Nothing about a full face helmet feels normal to me. It bears no sensory resemblance to any hat, eyeglasses, or earmuffs I have ever worn. Pressing against my cheekbones and forehead, hugging my entire skull and jawbone, the helmet narrows my field of vision and further restricts my hearing and tactile sensations. I can no longer feel the breeze in my thinning hair or the heat of the sun on my ears and face. The movement of my head is restricted, requiring me to turn my upper body to see what is beside me, yet I realize its protective advantages.

The final protective item I don before getting on my bike is a pair of leather gloves with gauntlets and padding in the palm and back of the fingers. These numb some of the feeling in my hands.

After putting on all my protective gear, my total encasement forces a readjustment of both mind and body. I am now incapacitated for actions of everyday life. I can't answer the phone, get money out of my pocket, check my email, or move lightly about the house. I am now prepared for action in an entirely different world.

The transformation through riding gear is both external and internal. Externally, I don't look like I'm ready to trim the lawn or take the kids to soccer practice. Suited up to ride, I have receded from the everyday world of my neighbors. I have become unknown, almost unknowable. Only my eyes and nose are visible, and then only up close. I find comfort in this complete disguise, not only when I ride to work, where few colleagues know that I'm a motorcyclist, but in general. In the daily struggle for freeway position, no one is aware of my age, race, or gender. Roadway glances reveal nothing about my looks, my facial expression, demeanor, or social status. If anything, a biker's garb provides misinformation through stereo-typing, suggesting that the person wearing it may be a rebel, outlaw, or a nonconformist who might be quick with his fists. Then again, the briefcase occasionally strapped on my seat probably suggests someone quick only with a fax.

Once I am fully attired in my garage, I swing my right leg over the bike's saddle, roll the bike off its center stand, and press the engine start button. Notched into first gear, the bike and I roll down my driveway toward the open canyon road.

While the gear I wear—my insurance against calamity—is indeed confining and cumbersome, its awkwardness and strangeness evaporate the moment I begin to ride. The weight of the garb becomes imper-ceptible, and what was anxiety-provoking is now reassuring. Before I travel a hundred yards, I enter a new world of experience in which my muted senses are an advantage not a deficit, allowing me to sense things in a new, heightened way. I am acutely aware of motion, balance, acceleration, and speed by the vibrations that radiate through the leather on my feet, hands, and torso. I feel the air on my face and smell the sage and eucalyptus through the helmet vents. I am aware of my environment in ways that rarely occur when I travel by car. Though my movement and senses are restricted by riding gear, I am transformed so I paradoxically experience intensified sensations rather than sensual deprivation—resulting in splendid isolation.

Mulholland Highway, near the Rock Store

5. Making Contact

THE KEY TO MOTORCYCLING is learning not to squander the eight square inches of rubber that connect motorcycle tires to the ground, referred to as the contact patch. Skilled motorcyclists think a lot about managing the two small patches, whereas drivers of autos generally never pay attention to them. There are many reasons for the difference—some readily apparent, others more subtle.

Motorcycle tires are relatively narrow and domed, compared to car tires, which are wide and flat. Their narrowness and shape permit only a small portion to be on the ground at any given moment. These design features are necessary for motorcycles to be turned easily, which requires that they be leaned into the direction of the curve in the road. These small contact patches carry a huge responsibility: transmitting the power to accelerate, providing the traction to stop, and allowing the bike to turn. The traction of the tires is a rider's Holy Grail. As soon as the rider begins to roll down the road, traction must be monitored as closely as a wallet on a bus in Rome.

Because of the importance of traction, all serious riders, regardless of their type of riding or brand of motorcycle, become connoisseurs of tires. Tire manufacturers vary the shapes and construction of their products, including the rubber compound used, attempting to maximize the traction for different types of motorcycling. There are tires for long-distance touring; for racetrack, street, or dirt riding; and for traveling in wet or dry environments. Softer rubber tires generally provide better traction but don't last very long. While typical car tires might last for forty thousand miles, those for motorcycles may last only one tenth as long. Their short lifespan is because while these softer, stickier tires enhance the motorcycle's ability to grasp the tarmac, in doing so they shred more quickly. Since riders' lives depend on the quality of the contact patch, tire purchases often constitute one of the most expensive maintenance costs.

Because traction is constantly in jeopardy, motor-cyclists are fanatic about tire pressure, too, checking it often. While seriously underinflated tires impede the ability to control a bike, too much pressure stiffens tires, making them less pliable and less capable of clinging to the contours of the road. Similarly, the temperature of tires as they heat up from use and outdoor conditions make a difference—warm tires grip better.

To assess potential performance of the contact patch, and thus safety, motorcyclists also become keen observers of road surfaces. A friend and highly skilled lifelong rider named Wendell was heading to the Rock Store early one morning. As he rounded a turn over a white rubberized crosswalk, which he had made hundreds of times, his front tire slipped because that morning the crossing was slightly moist from the coastal fog. Wendell crashed, damaging his favorite old BMW K100C, on which he had logged nearly one hundred thousand miles. In another incident, my friend Jim, riding a Beemer GS on one of his favorite mountain roads—the Angeles Crest Highway—did not see an oil spill on the new dark asphalt pavement. He got oil on his tires and, at the next corner, lost control immediately and totaled his bike. A car driver traveling those same roads would not have noticed anything hazardous or suffered a loss of traction. Fortunately, both riders were wearing full protective gear and were not seriously injured.

By nature, I am generally oblivious to my surroundings. My wife swears that she could redecorate the house and I wouldn't notice unless she drew it to my attention. But as a motorcyclist I rarely fail to spot a hazard in the road or note changes in the color or texture of pavement. I was forced to cultivate these powers of observation out of respect for the contact patch, which, if compromised in a way, could jeopardize traction. Paranoia in everyday life, involving the belief that everyone is out to get you, can be dysfunctional; but for motorcyclists, pavement paranoia is adaptive because everything on the road *is* out to get you. It is necessary to consider whether asphalt is new or old, rough or worn smooth; if there are bumps, potholes, or ruts that can cause a fall; and if there are road patches, manhole covers, or tar strips that could be slippery when wet or heated by the sun. Even features designed to increase highway safety can pose special risks for motorcyclists. For example, painted center lines, Botts dots (the small yellow plastic mounds between lanes in California), small reflectors glued to center lines, and crosswalk lines can all reduce traction because they are more slippery than the pavement and reduce the size of the contact patch momentarily by raising the tire. Momentary reductions in traction that occur when motorcycling at high speed or while turning can have serious consequences as well.

Animals crossing roads also pose special threats to maintaining traction. Unless they hit a cow, drivers of cars may feel a little squeamish in their squishy encounters with animals. For motorcyclists, however, even little critters can impede the job of the contact patch. I am constantly dodging squirrels, mice, gophers, snakes, rabbits, and quail as they scramble to dodge me. Encounters with larger animals, like deer, can be fatal. On a morning ride to the Rock Store, my friend Ryan T-boned a hapless wily coyote darting across the Mulholland Highway. More unusual, my buddy Peter had an encounter on the Angeles Crest Highway with a deer when it panicked and broadsided his motorcycle, putting an antler through his leather jacket and shoulder while he was riding. Nearly every weekend morning over coffee at the Rock Store someone had a fresh near-miss wildlife story to tell.

Few things reduce traction as quickly as water. When seeing a motorcyclist riding in the rain, nonriders have misplaced concern. Their reaction is usually, "Oh, you must get so wet," not realizing that with modern riding gear motorcyclists can ride for hours in the rain without getting wet. Rain does, however, pose a serious threat to traction. Even clean pavement can get unusually slippery during the first minutes of a rainstorm when the accumulated oil and grime seep from the asphalt and mix with the rain, producing a surface more like ice than pavement. This accounts for why, during the first rain after a long dry spell in Los Angeles, even cars lose some traction and unskilled and

careless drivers trade paint by the hundreds. Unfortunately for motorcyclists, we don't get away with minor
fender benders; we fall down and get injured. Even
worse, all the normal hazards for us—dirt, leaves,
manhole covers, lane lines—become doubly threatening when they are wet. This also happens with fog,
morning dew, runoff from sprinklers, and dampness
held in shady spots.

Just as important for maintaining traction as the
condition of the road surface is its shape, the frequency
and character of its turns. Before I became a motorcyclist, all highways seemed flat, and their turns were
nonevents. You simply moved the steering wheel a
bit with the fingers of one hand and around you went.
Even someone just learning to drive a car could master
it. However, turning a much smaller and lighter motorcycle is considerably more complicated. The shape and
condition of the road are central to maneuvering and
maintaining solid contact with the pavement. Cars
with their four wheels remain perpendicular to the
road when turning, while motorcycles can't turn if
they remain vertical and must be leaned at an angle.
Whereas modern suspension systems in cars attempt
to minimize leaning, leaning is essential for bikes. But
when they are leaned over, gravity threatens to pull
them down. Thus, paradoxically, to control a motorcycle it is necessary to learn to work with and against

gravity. There is a fine line between maintaining and losing control, and skilled motorcyclists master the management of that fine line. But many are not fully aware of how they actually turn their bikes and would have difficulty explaining it to a novice, although there are many detailed analyses of this process.[1]

You turn a bike not by turning the handlebars in the direction you want to go but by getting the bike to lean in that direction. There are two ways to accomplish this. The first way is intuitive but relatively ineffective: you shift your weight toward the turn with a little movement of your shoulders, butt, feet, or upper torso. This begins to lean and turn the bike a bit but would, by itself, be ineffective in making a sharp turn or any turn at a relatively high speed. The second way, which is counterintuitive but much more effective, is referred to as "counter-steering" and generates centrifugal forces that make the bike lean in the direction of the intended turn. With this method, you initiate a turn by simply pushing the handlebars for a split second in the direction *opposite* that in which you want to turn. Consider what would happen to a tall narrow truck that attempts to go around a left turn much too fast—the centrifugal force would cause it to

---

[1]See, for example, David L. Hough, *Proficient Motorcycling: The Ultimate Guide to Riding Well*, 2nd ed. (Irvine, CA: I-5 Press, 2008).

lean severely to the right, its left wheels nearly rising from the pavement, moments before it may fall over. It is precisely that seemingly dangerous kind of lean that a motorcyclist must initiate to turn, tricking the motorcycle by momentarily pushing the handlebars briefly in the opposite direction of the intended turn. Thus if the rider wants to make a right turn, he or she must get the bike to lean to the right by pushing the right handlebar forward an instant, making the front wheel go left momentarily. The bike will immediately "fall" to the right, at which point the rider must catch the lean, hold it constant, and ride around the right turn. That is why motorcyclists refer to turning as dropping into a corner with exactly the right amount of lean to make the turn while staying in their lane.

All turns nibble away at traction. At the very moments when you are making increased demands on the contact patch, the physics of turning reduces traction in proportion to the lean angle and speed. Thus even under the best circumstances taking corners is risky. As a result, skilled motorcyclists learn how to carefully read corners much as a bookie scrutinizes a racing sheet. The road camber, or slope, is one element that must be noted. Roads are often not flat in turns but banked, sloping down toward the inside of the turn. Banked corners naturally conserve traction by helping to lean the bike. In fact, on high-speed racetracks like

Daytona International Speedway, the steep-banked corners make race cars or motorcycles travel practically parallel to the ground with no loss of traction because the natural centrifugal forces that would normally throw the vehicle off the track are instead pressing the tires much more powerfully against the banked pavement. Motorcyclists love banked corners because they make leaning the bike easier, permitting greater speed without significantly threatening traction.

On the other hand, off-camber corners can be a nightmare. In off-camber corners the road surface slopes away from the direction of turn, colluding with the natural centrifugal forces in pushing the bike toward the outside of the turn, either off the road in left-handed corners or into oncoming traffic in right-handed turns. This is a potentially dangerous collusion of forces for the motorcyclist and requires a greater lean angle than on a flat road, reducing the traction. When combined with other hazards, like rain or gravel, off-camber turns must be taken at slower speed and with greater care.

Whatever the road surface or camber, the advice offered by experts is to "turn a corner only once." A rider should assess the corner before entry and select the quickest, safest, and smoothest way around it in one controlled motion. Novice riders have trouble doing this. Instead, they lean the bike as they enter a turn and then, finding that their lean angle is either too great or not great enough, they clumsily adjust it and, perhaps finding that their lean angle is still wrong, adjust it again before they exit the turn. Expert riders, by contrast, will drop the bike into precisely the right lean angle that allows them to hold the line throughout the curve and exit in one smooth, seemingly effortless arc.

Turning once is difficult enough to master even with constant-radius curves. But frequently, particularly on canyon or mountain roads, curves do not have a constant radius. Some turns begin in a tight corner and then open up, becoming less tight before straightening out again. More troublesome turns are those that have a decreasing radius; they start as sweet easy corners and then suddenly become sharper hair-raising turns. When motorcyclists are traveling below the posted speed limits, decreasing-radius turns present no particular problem; but when they are carving corners at a brisk clip, decreasing-radius turns present sudden technical difficulties requiring braking and changing lean angles simultaneously, pushing the tires to the limits of traction.

Blind corners that can't be assessed in advance pose challenges in proportion to the speed at which they are taken. Since riders can't see around such turns, they don't know the best line or speed for entering them and have to be mentally prepared for an unexpected decreasing-radius surprise that can quickly throw them off the road or into Farmer Fred's oncoming pickup truck. Blind corners require extra caution and an enhanced blend of skill, self-control, and faith, along with reduced speed and a wide arc to do reconnaissance on what's ahead.

There are many more technical aspects of taking corners that occupy skilled riders' minds, including the complexities of braking while leaned over, the effects of approaching curves when the elevation is rapidly rising or falling, the subtleties of establishing a line through a corner before entering it, using the bike's gears to control compression braking. All these cognitive and physical calculations must be tightly choreographed for the few seconds it takes to approach, enter, and exit curves. On unfamiliar canyon, country, and mountain roads, every curve is different, and each one requires a customized mental and physical strategy. In a morning of weekend riding on twisty roads with my buddies, we might confront a thousand different turns, coming one after another at five- to fifteen-second intervals. The pinnacle of riding expertise is to be able to make these thousand calculations instinctively. It demands full concentration and razor-sharp skills—the definitive test of mastery.

All turns put motorcyclists on edge—the edge of tires, the edge of traction, the edge of catastrophe. The risks, magnified exponentially with increased speed, must be confronted in nanoseconds and managed with craftsmanship-like skill. Then the reward can be a graceful ballet of man, machine, and nature, an experience on the edge of transcendence.

Latigo Canyon Road, Malibu, California

6. Near Tragedy on a Twisty Knot of a Road

ONE OF THE JOYS of riding well is the requirement of melding physical dexterity and mental alertness. However, when the delicate balance between these major aspects of biking is not maintained calamity can occur. Once, on a biker's perfect Sunday summer morning I set off on a ride. There was no sign of the low fog that had been hugging the coast. The sun was already warm as it crested the mountain, promising to get hot by the time most people stumbled out to get the newspaper. I planned to ride on my R1100RS on Latigo Canyon Road to the Rock Store, eager to gather with those more serious about motorcycle talk than the quality of the coffee.

Latigo Canyon Road spiraled up the canyon west of my home in Southern California's dry Santa Monica Mountains. When I first moved there from New

York and inquired at Marty's Beemer shop about the best twisty roads, it was one of the first roads mentioned. It is an infamous 10-mile, 194-turn road that once was the site of road races among the young sport bike set before the police intervened. There are never many cars on it early on Sunday mornings because it is a road only a motorcyclist could love. It rises from the Pacific beach, snaking instantly up the sage- and cactus-covered mountainside, providing breathtaking peeks of the ocean as it climbs through canyons to nearly two thousand feet. It's a second-gear ride all the way, from the hairpin corners cut through the chaparral to the brief straightaways along canyon edges. As it winds through the hills, it throws every kind of corner at you: beautifully banked and paved curves, gravelly domed off-camber challenges, increasing-radius and decreasing-radius turns. The road climbs and falls several times over the mountains, meandering out of and then back into canyons. One minute you are in the cool morning shade; a moment later in the bright warmth of the day. But the early morning sun can be a major impediment to swiftness, blinding you in eastward-turning corners as it rises above the mountain ridge.

I vowed to ride at a judicious but spirited pace, staying within my limits, remembering the previous weekend's group ride up the coast above Santa Barbara, where, as we later confessed, we rode too fast. As I rode, I kept my pace comfortable yet interesting. I was in no hurry, but I wasn't exactly sightseeing either. I was riding and thinking about riding simultaneously: What a glorious morning with a perfect temperature, what an exquisite road, what magnificent vistas and enormously fun tight and narrow corners, I thought. I was considering how I would describe it in writing to those who had never been blessed by its beauty or smelled the dusty fragrance of this desert mountain.

I was near the top end of Latigo Canyon Road, a quarter-mile from where it joins Kanan-Dume Road, just a few minutes from my first cup of coffee. "'A twisty knot of a road'—that is how to describe Latigo Canyon Road," I said proudly to myself as I leaned into an easy 30 mph downhill right-hander. At that very instant, I was pounded. My right foot slammed against the pavement in a reflex action, completely out of my control. My bike's front end went left and hammered right, also seemingly without my deliberation or input, as it first slid out and then regained traction. Instead of landing in the right lane on my butt as the bike skidded on its right side in a low-sider, or on my head as the bike slid then abruptly "stood up," casting me off the road on the left side in what is euphemistically referred to as a "high-sider," the bike miraculously regained its composure, stayed with the rubber side down, and rolled awkwardly through the corner as I brought it to a slow stop, trying to regain my composure, which had vanished while I thought for certain I was going down.

"What the hell happened?" I asked myself, gasping. I was momentarily stunned by the suddenness of how my comfortable ride had nearly become a disaster, frightened by what could have happened on this isolated road, angry at myself for having failed to avoid this trauma, and uncertain about what to do next. Shaking, I carefully dismounted and checked my bike for damage. I could see none, but then I was not seeing or thinking very clearly at that moment. I noticed that my ankle felt slightly sprained, but otherwise the damage appeared to be primarily psychological. Only several hours later did I register the pain in my lower back and my sore right wrist, which for many weeks would serve as a reminder of my unexpected loss of control and near disaster.

I turned the bike around and rode warily back to examine the site of this near calamity, intending to search for an explanation, find some cheap reassurance. The road preceding the corner was bathed in bright sunlight, but as the road turned into the blind right-hander, the point where I had dropped the bike into a lean, the pavement sank into a deep shadow. There, just inside the shadow, in the middle of the right lane, lay a five-inch-wide, five-foot-long mixture of sand

and fine gravel and, at its center, the evidence—the imprint of my front tire.

Although I was accustomed to these canyon roads and the loose gravel that frequently descended on them, I had not seen this common hazard at all. I would like to claim that the hazard could not have been foreseen, given the sharp curve of the descending road and the light-to-shadow transition, making it impossible to avoid the mishap. I would like to claim that as careful as we all might be there still remain dangers we cannot entirely escape. As a generalization, this is true, and all serious riders live with these risks. But, unfortunately, it was not true in my case. The gravel, albeit partially hidden, was visible enough. The accident had been due to my error, not nature's trickery.

There is a very thin line between a splendid excursion and tragedy. That line can be erased by a simple roadside distraction, a momentary lapse in judgment, or the intrusion of a disquieting thought or emotion, anything that interferes with the delicate balance between physical dexterity and mental alertness that must be maintained. For me, contemplating writing about that wonderful twisty knot of a road—thinking about it instead of watching it—had interfered with riding it skillfully and mindfully.

The image of speed

7. Speed
A Wily, Addictive Temptress

SPEED IS THE WILY, addictive temptress of motor-cyclists. It can transform a beautiful curve into a gruesome nightmare, an elegantly designed motorcycle into scrap metal, and a mild-mannered middle-aged man into an organ donor. When I resumed riding at age forty-five, I told myself that speed was the great escalator of risk, a loaded gun in the drawer—dangerous, life-threatening, and unnecessary. I vowed to avoid it. It was an easy promise to make because speed scared me, so it was like giving up liver for Lent. Speed wasn't important, I reasoned; it was the freedom of the ride that was to be cherished. Speed was a little boy's thrill, an adolescent's mindless obsession, not a thinking man's pursuit.

I was soon forced to drop the pretense. I found myself going fast too often, seeking swiftness like a drug, relishing its rush. I had to face the obvious fact that speed, along with the risks that accompanied it, was at the core of sport riding, part of what Melissa Holbrook Pierson, in her book *The Perfect Vehicle*, referred to as the "precious danger" of motorcycling.

Speed furnishes a good part of the thrill of riding. Motion at any rate faster than a walk—whether on a merry-go-round, train, roller-coaster, car, bicycle, or backyard swing—can be exhilarating. From infancy we like being swooped around by caretakers, enjoying the strange but intoxicating mixture of motion and controlled fear. There is something transcendent about rapid motion, something seductive, bordering on being addictive.

Yet among motorcyclists speed, although a crude and imperfect measure, is also the standardized test of riding skill—imperfect because merely going fast can be a sign of either skill or stupidity. Speed on straightaways can be obtained by riders of all skill levels; it merely indicates their willingness to risk the sudden crossing of a deer or an SUV. On such a road, anyone with the ability to climb on a motorcycle and twist their wrist can get a motorcycle to go 100 mph in a few seconds. But those who are truly skilled are distinguished from the reckless as soon as the road turns sharply and requires one to orchestrate the necessary symphony of subtle quick moves: successfully set the timing, pick the line, shift, brake, lean, and accelerate in a few seconds in one smooth, flowing motion. Less-skilled riders underestimate the expertise required to keep a heavy machine from careening off the road. When riders unwisely try to ride above their skill level, they invariably draw the unwanted attention of emergency medical personnel, police, and insurance agents.

A twisty road provides the essential measure of motorcycling skill. In determining such skill, social demographics and wealth are irrelevant. On a curvy road, a bike's cost, horsepower, or aftermarket equipment matter not a whit. A skilled veteran rider on a cheap old bike can easily leave a young unskilled rider on a new, more expensive, and powerful bike in the dust. In the flash of two corners, a pauper can rise above a prince in the world of riding. The ability to control a motorcycle on a challenging road is the coin of the realm, the marker of riding skill.

The capitals of this realm are the coffee shops that serve as gathering spots for motorcyclists—from Marcus Dairy in Connecticut to Newcomb's Ranch in the mountains high above Los Angeles—where, amidst the chatter about tire compound and rebound damping, many (myself among them) tend to exaggerate their riding skills and imagine themselves consummate canyon racers.

In Sport Bike America, there is no way to distinguish the podium finisher from the poseur. At the
Rock Store I have sipped bad coffee from a Styrofoam
cup while standing next to a former superbike world
champion, and I doubt that anyone who didn't know
us could have easily identified who the champion
was. This ambiguity evokes both the charm of these
settings and the anxiety that comes from uncertainty.
However, whatever status ambiguity exists among
riders in such places ends as soon as a group begins to
ride together. In a single twisty mile, everyone's level
of skill—displayed as a combination of speed and
control—is apparent, and the riding order is sorted
out as the more skilled riders advance to the front.
Just as an expert in tennis can distinguish a pro from
an amateur by observing a few volleys, and an expert
in surfing can distinguish a pro from an amateur by
watching people catch a few waves, a motorcyclist can
estimate another's level of skill by following him or
her through a few turns. The ability to deftly manage
speed though a turn cannot be faked any better than
a novice violinist attempting to sound like a concert
master. Skill assigns everyone to their place.

As much as I try to deny it, the competition for
place is keen. When a new rider appears, no one cares
who she or he is in the nonbiker world. The only per-
tinent question is: How well does the person ride on

a twisty road? And the answer to this question determines the individual's social status in the sport bike world. Unfortunately, seeking status through speed without control often produces grim results along mountain and canyon roads.

Even experienced, skilled riders may get themselves in trouble with speed when they lack self-discipline. Safe riding is the result of controlling intoxicating feelings: there is the exhilaration of speed itself, the heightened anticipation that engulfs the rider as he or she rushes toward the next corner, the embedded competitiveness of group rides, the pressure on the lead rider to set a swift pace and on the slowest not to be left behind, and the feeling of inadequacy that can emerge from measuring your skills against those of others. Additionally, there is that grab bag of chaotic emotions from your personal life—hurt, anger, jealousy, frustration—that can be distracting as you ride. Recognizing and keeping these emotions in check is as much a part of riding skill as the ability to grind a foot peg in a tight corner.

The potential danger of speed's seductiveness coupled with a mix of toxic emotions was brought home to me one day while riding my familiar forty-five-minute route to my office in Los Angeles. I generally think of myself as a reasonably stable adult and a thoughtful rider. But on this Tuesday morning at 7:00 I began to act increasingly like a maniac. As with many others, I didn't like the Los Angeles traffic and freeways, yet riding my bike to work usually ameliorated the unpleasant experience, bootlegged some fun into the daily grind. But on this day as I rolled onto the crowded freeway, a different me took over. I became quickly irritated by the size of the vehicles that blocked my view and by the careless way drivers were handling their cars. Overcome by a stupid sense of superiority, I began to think the drivers were unworthy to share the road with me. As I moved from lane to lane and between cars (lane splitting is legal in California), passing scores of road-ragers, I began to fear that each resentful driver I passed was a rolling assassin assigned to snuff me out. Simultaneously, my sense of competitiveness surfaced, and I became an alien racer from a different universe, darting past the caged beings applying their makeup, talking on their cell phones, drinking their coffee—and endangering me if I slowed too much. This onslaught of emotional irrationality and the desire for greater speed had clearly impaired my judgment.

The problem is not about going fast per se but about allowing the emotions of riding to push you into going faster and less cautiously than your skills warrant. On the infamous Angeles Crest Highway, where there are more than a few motorcyclist deaths a year, the common suspicion among older riders is that young "squids" allow testosterone to impair their judgment and adolescent machismo to overwhelm their riding skills. One could dismiss these criticisms as little more than older riders' envy of youth and their carefree daring—claims to which there may be some truth. Even so, serious older riders have managed to stay alive for decades by recognizing the importance of mastering not just their machines but also themselves.

Crashing is always unexpected and unwanted, something riders failed to avoid—usually due to lack of skill or going too fast—and therefore seemingly epitomizing lack of control. But, interestingly, the expressions riders use to describe crashing imply control. For example, one morning Ben, a skilled motorcyclist, offered to let me ride his tricked-out R1100S. "Don't throw it away" was Ben's only advice as I mounted his fine motorcycle to depart. By using the admonition "Don't throw it away," Ben was suggesting that crashing was controllable and his preference was that I not choose to do it on his bike.

Motorcyclists' rhetoric about crashing is full of such linguistic manipulations: he laid his bike down; he got off; he tossed his bike; he threw it down. Such phrases represent more than the slang that accompanies sports in general. Rather, they transform the act of losing control to something the rider actively chooses, deemphasizing the unpredictability and chaos

of crashing and instead seeing the potential of crashing as another opportunity to display mastery by
overcoming the temptation to ride at a speed beyond
one's control. Speed is indeed a wily, addictive temptress, but the addiction must be carefully managed to
become more instructive than the childlike thrill of
motion or the primal assertion of male competitiveness. Speed should be employed to indicate mastery of
the art of motorcycling and mastery of self.

Two yellow lines

8. Crossing the Double Yellow

OVER COFFEE AT THE ROCK STORE one weekend morning Ryan sheepishly confessed that he had gotten a missive from Officer Friendly while traveling on Highway 150, one of our favorite twisty roads into the east end of Ojai. The infraction was for crossing the double yellow line while passing a cluster of cars. What disappointed us was not the ticket itself but the fact that Ryan was driving a car at the time instead of riding one of his motorcycles.

Even as a repeat offender, I admit that there are good reasons for enforcing laws about the right-of-way, speed limits, driving while intoxicated, signaling before turning, stopping for red lights and stop signs, and so forth. Motorists should be grateful when they see highway warning signs to slow down for upcoming road construction, narrow bridges, deer crossings, or

unexpected sharp turns in the road, all of which are
designed to protect drivers from their own poor judgment and from each other. But although the laws
are reasonable and the penalties for breaking them
often stiff, violations are widespread. Perhaps in no
other realm of activity do so many people share a
public record as offenders, demonstrating a remarkable
display of public misbehavior. These offenses are not
motivated by a desire for economic gain, as they are in
the pervasive fudging of income tax returns. Nor do
they stem from antipathy toward fellow travelers. And
clearly they don't arise from any grassroots political
rebellion, deliberate expressions of civil disobedience,
or recrimination against the state. Instead, they arise
from mundane ignorance, lack of skill, carelessness,
and haste.

As Ryan discovered, one traffic offense is potentially momentous: failure to stay in the proper lane.
Because vehicles traveling in opposite directions zoom
past each other only a few yards apart at a combined
speed difference that may exceed 120 mph, there is
good reason to keep these streams of traffic segregated.
In fact, most interstate highways are built with formida-
ble barriers separating such potential antagonists. But
physical separation is generally not possible on two-
lane byways. Here drivers become impatient when
following an inordinately slow vehicle, perhaps that

of an elderly couple summoning courage to make their way down an unfamiliar road or a truck lumbering up a grade. Traffic engineers, recognizing the impulse of swift drivers to use the oncoming lane to pass slower ones, opted not to forbid it but to carefully regulate it. A dashed center line is a concession to the impatient driver, a state-sanctioned opportunity to cross over momentarily into banned territory. This permission, however, is contingent on the visibility ahead, the absence of oncoming traffic, the capacity of the vehicle, and the skill of the driver to quickly pass and return to the right lane. Where there is insufficient visibility, a solid single or double yellow line prohibits passing. So serious is this admonition that the penalties for crossing it are more severe than for other traffic infractions. In California, for example, the penalties are considerably more punitive than those for a speeding ticket, and two such infractions can jeopardize your driver's license, a fate on a par with castration in our car-obsessed culture.

Since the consequences of a head-on crash are dramatic and the penalties steep, it is not surprising that among drivers this prohibition against crossing the double yellow line may be the most obeyed traffic law. But among motorcyclists it is probably the least obeyed traffic law. This difference reveals an important aspect of motorcycling as a sport.

For bikers, crossing the yellow line is not an infraction committed by outcasts, as suggested by the American stereotype of motorcyclists. In fact, the serious motorcyclist is more likely to be a policeman or an attorney than a hoodlum. (Some of my pals would say they don't see the distinction.) Most motorcyclists in general are not prone to disregard traffic laws and, like other motorists, stay within wavering range of the speed limit, signal when turnings, and stop when lights turn red. But traffic saints they are not. They can be as careless as other motorists and certainly earn their proportion of traffic citations. But when it comes to crossing the double yellow line, motorcyclists flagrantly, frequently, and deliberately ignore it.

There are good explanations for such disobedience. The first explanation is that the double yellow line is "autocentric," created with the performance of cars in mind. Solid or dashed center lines—the product of simple algorithms of the sight distance available, presumed traveling speed, the capacity of the average car to accelerate, and the ability of the average driver to pass another vehicle safely—are based on a formula developed for four-wheel vehicles. Most motorcycles can accelerate much faster than all but a few exotic race cars. Many of today's sport motorcycles weigh less than five hundred pounds, have between one hundred and two hundred horsepower, and can accelerate from

0 to 60 mph in less than four seconds. The horsepower-to-weight ratio of motorcycles far exceeds that of all automobiles, allowing them to pass in a fraction of the time and distance required by cars, and thereby posing no great risk. Thus the double yellow line is an inaccurate and largely useless warning for motorcyclists, many of whom consequently view crossing the yellow line as a personal statement about the irrelevance of this injunction and a protest against the unjustifiable restraint it creates. This explanation was only partially appreciated by the Ventura County sheriff who had a little chat with four of us (including Ryan) on the same road where Ryan had been ticketed a year earlier. Apparently, there was something about our crossing a double yellow line and traveling at double the posted speed limit that had piqued his interest. Miraculously, no citations were issued.

The second explanation for such disobedience by motorcyclists is that the double yellow line suppresses part of the essence of riding. Motorcyclists don't cross the double yellow line because they are in a hurry—to slice a few minutes off a trip to the mall or to get home to watch a ball game—as car drivers do. In fact, motorcyclists are as motivated to get to a destination on time as downhill skiers are to get to the bottom of a hill, or surfers to the shore. Usually, motorcyclists ride to experience the thrill of mastering a finely engineered machine and the exhilaration of traveling swiftly and smoothly over twisty, demanding roads.

The interstate highway system—the flat, straight, multilane grid that crisscrosses the nation—is a great boon to motorcyclists but not because they like it. The benefit of the interstate highway system is that it attracts drivers, keeping them off the backcountry two-lane blacktop that is the playground for motorcyclists. Motorcyclists love the roads that others hate, the ones full of unrelenting curves demanding full concentration, on which a momentary lapse of attention or judgment can result in a week of dining on hospital food and, even less savory, spending time with insurance agents. These are often the roads that have not single but double yellow lines, prohibiting passing in either direction for many, many miles. The roads that stir motorcyclists' souls the most transform motorcycle riding into an aesthetic in which mind, matter, and machine become one flowing experience, on which every corner is an opportunity for gravity-defying mastery, for a test of mental concentration and physical dexterity, for immersion in the exhilaration that comes from the sharp edge of risk.

Such exhilaration can only be achieved when cornering "at speed," at a brisk pace. Motorcyclists take corners leaned over and traveling faster than cars, which, although a technical requirement, also provides the thrill of riding well. If they are stuck behind a slow car on a twisty road, it is impossible to ride well, meaningfully, or enjoyably. In fact, on the best stretches of twisty roads with double yellow lines, a slow car doesn't only prevent enjoyment for a turn or two; it threatens to nullify the potentially exhilarating experience offered by a marvelous road that may go on for several miles and hundreds of curves. Riding behind such a vehicle is comparable to attending a concert unable to hear, going to a ballet blindfolded, or being served the finest gourmet cuisine immediately after suffering through oral surgery. The sudden realization that you are trapped behind a slow car on heaven's road can be an emotional calamity, and the need for liberation is instantaneous and powerful.

Such moments—when double yellow lines conspire with slow cars to enforce irrelevant prohibitions—are when disobedience becomes imperative for motorcyclists. "Crossing the double yellow" then signifies that they march to the beat of a different drummer, that they refuse to forfeit their opportunity for exhilaration to two yellow lines.

Clashing mirrors

9. Lane Splitting in La-La Land

NOT LONG AFTER I BEGAN RIDING a motorcycle
I discovered that while I might be sharing the
road with cars going in the same direction at approx-
imately the same speed, my ways of traversing the
landscape were different. This was particularly the case
in California, where the contrasts are readily apparent
in motorcyclists' pervasive practice of lane splitting.
Bikers lane split when they commandeer the vacant
spaces between car lanes as they weave through, using
whatever gaps may be available.

This traffic maneuver, while legal and encouraged
in most countries, is illegal in North America, with
the exception of the risk-tolerant, fire-and-earthquake
state of California. There, in a triumph of legislative
ambivalence, lane splitting is officially neither legal
nor illegal but rather left to the proper authorities to

determine, instance by instance, if it was done "safely." Motorcyclists in California exploit the ambiguity so extensively that they have come to think that the right to lane split should be an amendment to the US Constitution, up there with the right to vote or speak freely. They also regard it as a public health benefit, considering it the only way to get through clogged freeways without going crazy, a frequent mental state of frustrated drivers.

So enamored are bikers of this maneuver that they euphemistically call it "lane sharing." But while it is occurring neither riders nor car drivers are actually lane sharing. A more accurate though less socially acceptable term would be "space hijacking" or "space exploitation" since it is more like the unauthorized occupation of abandoned buildings by urban squatters than a cooperative joint activity.

Chief among those who benefit from lane splitting are motorcyclists who have the appropriate skills. On streets, they can save considerable time by lane splitting at stop signs and stoplights, which allows them to jump ahead of many cars. Additionally, to save time on packed multilane freeways, which, in congested urban areas, can extend for many miles, lane splitting helps them stream between slow-moving cars. I mastered these maneuvers during my twenty years of commuting and riding around Los Angeles, sarcastically referred to as La-La Land, often shaving about thirty minutes off a trip.

Lane splitting has unrecognized benefits for drivers, too. In states where the practice is prohibited, a motorcycle is required to occupy a car's worth of space in a line of vehicles. In cities with many motorcycle commuters, the lines at stop signs and stoplights and on clogged freeways, made longer by motorcycles occupying so much space, are relieved of congestion by allowing them in the vacant spaces between lines.

Accordingly, you would think that drivers would applaud lane splitters for saving them some time, but instead drivers are often annoyed by lane splitters. Drivers usually offer the bogus objection that they are concerned about motorcyclists' safety. Lane splitting often looks risky to drivers who are passed at close range, and when lane splitting is done too rapidly, carelessly, or unskillfully, it can actually be dangerous. But according to recent California studies lane splitting may not be as dangerous as car drivers imagine.[2] Besides, driving a car too rapidly, carelessly, or unskillfully is also dangerous. Actually, distracted, careless, unskilled drivers are the major safety threat to riders, lane splitting or not.

---

[2] See *Rider Magazine* (January 2015): 11; "Preview: SafeTREC Motorcycle Collision Study," *CityBike* (July 2014): 3–4; and "Splitting Headache: 2014 OTS Lane Share Survey," *CityBike* (August 2014): 6.

After twenty years of freeway traveling, I've seen it all: drivers frequently changing lanes without signaling or glancing over their shoulder; aggressively moving into my lane, causing me to quickly get out of their way; texting, drinking, or eating with both hands; reading, shaving, or applying makeup. I once witnessed a car driver working on a crossword puzzle and a truck driver smoking from a large bong, using both hands. If the driving public was truly concerned about motorcyclists' safety, it would curb its own negligent habits.

California drivers' objection to lane splitting, it seems, isn't really about concern for the safety of motorcyclists but about privilege and unfairness. This is California, the kingdom of big, expensive cars and drivers with high estimates of their own social prominence, many of whom perceive motorcyclists as lower-class rogues, bad-assed scofflaws—and, admittedly, a few probably deserve the designation. When self-important drivers see assumed hooligans getting ahead of them in traffic, they think of it as cheating at their expense. And as they stew in the juices of urban congestion they suffer an additional affront to their sense of entitlement, an insult by low-life riders advancing to the front of the line, failing to recognize the drivers' privileged status. Thus lane splitting by motorcyclists appears to car drivers as an unfair and disrespectful advantage, as if riders were flipping them the bird while they weaseled past, an activity that annoyed car drivers think should be prohibited.

Actually, lane splitters are much too preoccupied to be conveying insults since they face a confluence of details that must be managed from one moment to the next. Certainly, lane splitting up to a traffic light between stopped cars requires nothing more than riding in a straight line without weaving too much. However, the challenge of lane splitting when vehicles are in motion, perhaps at 30 or 40 mph, is much more demanding. Lane splitters must stare ahead at a closing funnel of opportunity as they view openings in the long line of cars ahead. If riders are moving about 10 mph faster than the cars, they are passing between cars every second or two while the funnel of opportunity is constantly morphing; the cars on the left may be traveling at a different speed than those on the right; cars may be weaving within their lanes rather than moving in unison, creating constantly fluctuating distances between adjacent cars. Taking all these factors into account, riders must then anticipate when there might be sufficient gaps between cars to safely lane split. Also, mirrors typically protrude a few inches on each side of bikes and perhaps a foot on cars and trucks. Riders have an intuitive sense of the placement of their own mirrors, but others' mirrors are at different heights, requiring riders to make instantaneous assessments of whether the left and right mirrors on their bikes will pass below, above, or "clip" the car mirrors, possibly breaking them if the space becomes too narrow at the last second. Saddlebags present additional complications.

Seasoned lane splitters are fully preoccupied making such calculations with every pass. They are considering such questions as: Is there enough space to squeeze by? Will the next two cars ahead be side-by-side or not exactly adjacent when I pass between them? Are the two cars going the same speed or different speeds? Are their speeds changing or likely to change given the brake lights up ahead? Are the drivers distracted? Are the cars wandering in their respective lanes, perhaps preparing to change lanes? How do all the mirrors line up? Do I need to speed up or slow down to make the pass safely? If this sounds difficult and potentially risky, it is. It's not for the novice or the negligent.

Lane spitting skills are mastered gradually, and the learning curve is different for everyone, a balancing of desire and caution, aspiration and skill, impatience and perseverance. At some point, lane splitters who have become proficient at this technique realize that instantaneous computations about speed, distance, space, and simultaneous movements of lines of cars, calculations revised every second for miles on end, assessments on which safety depends, have become nearly automatic and achieved almost unconsciously, much as a professional baseball batter who in fractions of a second makes decisions about whether or where to swing at 100 mph pitches—except that lane splitters can't afford to swing and miss.

While lane splitting provokes in car drivers a strange mix of fear and loathing, as well as envy and jealousy,[3] motorcyclists who lane split relish the opportunity to seize wasted territory and publicly demonstrate their superior status in the urban traffic game.

---

[3]Mark Taylor and Jose Marquez, "Cycles of Paradox," in Guggenheim Museum, *The Art of the Motorcycle* (1998): 33–34.

Santa Monica, California

10. Dead of Night Departure

THE THRILL, tinged with apprehension, felt when departing in the dead of night for a long motor-cycle trip is exhilarating and unforgettable. On one of my first such adventures, afraid of arriving late for the departure and generally apprehensive about the trip, I awoke even earlier than necessary. Carol Ann, unaccustomed to having me depart in the middle of the night, expressed concern about the ride. I told her not to worry, that I'd be back in about a week. As I left the bedroom, she mumbled sleepily, "Be careful. I love you."

"I'll be fine," I replied. I understood her concerns, realizing that she could not know my exact where-abouts, only that for a day or so I would be somewhere in Colorado.

As I traveled down the canyon road from my home in the coastal mountains of Southern California to the meeting place at Dolores's Café in Santa Monica that foggy July night, I had the Pacific Coast Highway to myself. Knowing I could be regarded as suspicious by being the only vehicle on the highway, I wondered how I would explain myself if stopped by the only other motorist I passed, a county sheriff. This biking mission had been planned months before, but the sparse details had been worked out only in the past days, in a few brief meetings and phone calls. I did not know exactly who I was to accompany until the evening I left. But I didn't really need to know. None of us did. It was less complicated that way.

I arrived early. I had never been at Dolores's Café. "Two blocks west of the 405. Be there at 3:00 am, ready to go," was all I had been told.

When I entered, my friend Jim was there alone. Had he cultivated a flowing white beard to accompany his silver hair, portly shape, and red outfit, he might have passed for an off-season Santa Claus. A movie film editor by day, he had recently returned from Ireland, where he had been on a three-month shoot. He glanced at me with a knowing smile. Not much had to be said. I gave the empty place a quick once-over, slid in beside him in the window booth, and ordered a cup of coffee and stale pastry from the tired waitress.

After a while, Jim and I were joined in the café by three young hookers. They were animated and convivial, showing a relief that must have come from the completion of a night's risky work. Perhaps put off by our attire, they showed no interest in us, although they had to know our type: men with graying hair, furtive eyes, and awkward uneasiness about being there at that time of night. Also disinterested, we were quiet and solemn due to our interrupted night's sleep and focusing our thoughts on the trip ahead.

A few minutes later Ryan, an adrenaline junkie, arrived from the San Fernando Valley. A successful entrepreneur and owner of a photographic business in his public life, he was eagerly relishing this middle-of-the-night excursion. Quick with irreverent one-liners, he needed no coffee to be quipping, "Killed anything yet?" This provided us with a needed emotional release.

Our anticipation rose as Joel, the manager of a car dealership in the South Bay, arrived. With his meticulously coifed silver-streaked hair and black attire, he resembled a character from *The Godfather*. He was by far the most experienced at these nighttime adventures, while for me it was an anxiety-filled first trial. He showed no anxiety, or any interest in delaying our departure.

With Joel's arrival, it was time to go. A gang of four was an optimum number—not so many individuals as to impede our timetable and enough to handle any problems if something went wrong. We were a totally unexpected group; we had never traveled together. No one in our public lives would have connected us, and only a few would ever understand our motivation.

We accepted Jim's lead. A loner by choice, his abilities in our small circle were legendary. He was the person among us who would not have hesitated to go alone and perhaps preferred it since it was easier, less complicated, and quicker to travel that way. His wife, accustomed to him leaving quietly in the middle of the night, had stopped worrying about him. He was the kind of man her father, a physician who had witnessed carnage, had warned her to avoid.

We departed together in silence, alone in our private thoughts as we left Los Angeles, heading east. The I-10 Freeway, the most heavily traveled road in the nation, was eerily empty. As we escaped from the LA Basin, we increased our speed. We flew past Palm Springs and Indio and out into the desert, in a race with the desert heat, expected to climb to nearly 120 degrees by midday, at which time we hoped to be across the wasteland and in the mountains of northern Arizona.

We neither stopped nor spoke to each other for the rest of the night. Glances or simple gestures were all that was needed. We were together but very much alone in our own private worlds, each studying the blurred darkness surrounding us and the blinking stream of white lines below.

Our spirits rose dramatically as soon as we were underway, and the farther we went the more in sync we each became with the mission. The venture quickly took on a life of its own and engulfed us in a world far from filmmaking, or from the selling of photographic equipment or cars, or from teaching. Our public lives rapidly receded in the smoky night haze of Southern California.

Dawn in the desert was magnificent, with muted hues and gentle light. The desert around us, glimpsed only by moonlight for hours, became increasingly visible, restoring sight to us. The odor of sage filled the land all the way to the mesas on the horizon.

As a lonely gas station appeared, we simultaneously started gearing down our BMW motorcycles from their 100 mph cruising speed for our first stop. When we took our full face helmets and leather jackets off, we all beamed ear to ear. At this stop to refuel, we could finally revel in our escape. We were as revved as four fifty-year-old men ever get.

The excuse for the trip was a national gathering of BMW motorcyclists in Durango, Colorado, but for serious riders like us no excuse was needed, as riding is its own consuming experience and reward. Considering motorcycling a mode of transportation to get somewhere is about as accurate as thinking of a rare tapestry as a means of covering walls, or seeing Olympic diving as a way to go swimming—it completely missed the point. Of course, there are those for whom motorcycles are merely an inexpensive mode of transportation. And there are those for whom motorcycles are merely acquisitions of status, interchangeable with Rolex watches, sport utility vehicles, swimming pools, and Armani suits, something they "own" not something they do passionately, and largely without their casual acquaintances even knowing. Things people possess as status symbols, tend not to gain a prominent place in their emotional lives, absorb most of their free time, or interfere with their vacation planning. By contrast, motorcycling as a sport possesses serious riders.

Riding as a sport is a diversion, a respite from whatever otherwise occupies a person's time. Like surfing or tennis, it involves physical skill and exertion. And like most pastimes it requires persistence and practice to master. But sport riding is different from these in at least two major respects: few other sports involve becoming one with a complex machine or running the constant risk of serious injury or worse due to a momentary lapse of concentration or a simple misjudgment of your own skill. Motorcycling as a sport is more akin to rock and mountain climbing, hang gliding, and skiing.

It demands agility, concentration, and the integrated use of mind and body.

Motorcycle riding, like other sports, is engaged in for many different reasons. Some riders are mere dabblers, using their bikes occasionally to run a short errand in the neighborhood. Some commuters use motorcycles as a cheap means of transportation to work and would not think of spending a weekend or their free time on their bikes. Others, who have large touring bikes, such as the nearly thousand-pound Honda Gold Wing, may use their motorcycles once or twice a year for a week or longer tour, a two-wheel equivalent of a trip in an RV. And for many owners of "cruisers," like the Harley-Davidson motorcycles that garner the media's attention, the bikes themselves are a cultural symbol of rebellion, even though their owners increasingly are as likely to be ensconced in chairs at the local coffee bar sipping decaf nonfat double lattes as perched on bar stools in a sleazy joint swigging Jack Daniels. But for none of these motorcyclists is riding a sport with the goal of mastery.

Nor was it for me when, suddenly and unexpectedly, in late fall 1990 I decided as a forty-five-year-old college professor to purchase a motorcycle and resume motorcycling. To this day, I don't fully understand my inspiration for returning to riding, although the convenient cover could have been a midlife crisis, had I

not already had several. I hadn't set foot in a motorcycle shop in decades; I hadn't known a single rider;
I had paid absolutely no attention to the world of
motorcycling since my youth; I had never read a moto
magazine. I had been living in Manhattan, hardly a
motorcycling-friendly environment, and I hadn't ridden
a motorcycle in over twenty years, and then it was a
small Yamaha 80, followed by a "you meet the nicest
people" Honda, which I used solely to commute a few
miles to campus. To my mind, motorcycles in those
days had cost only a few hundred dollars, weighed
about two hundred pounds, and were never ridden
outside the city or over 40 mph, or considered anything more than a cheap way to climb the Berkeley
hills without pedaling.

However, once I made the decision in mid-life to
start looking for a motorcycle, my life was transformed
in ways I never anticipated. I began subscribing to
more motorcycle magazines than professional and
scientific journals. I began spending more money on
motorcycle leathers and gear than I ever did on double-
breasted wool suits and silk ties. My friends at the time
were all New York academics, all in one department, all
with similar backgrounds and outlooks. My nonriding
acquaintances had the same perplexed expression on
their faces when they learned that I rode a motorcycle.

My newfound absorption in riding was difficult to explain.

By now, decades later, I have ridden nearly half a million miles up and down the East and West Coasts on thirty different motorcycles. Yet I have never forgotten the thrill and apprehension I felt during that dead of night escape from mundane life through motorcycling.

PART THREE

ADAPTING TO THE CYCLES OF LIFE

Highway 33, above Ojai, California

11. The Grabbers of Santa Barbara

MOVING FROM NEW YORK to Los Angeles was advantageous in a number of ways, as I had hoped. I was once again located very close to my son and daughter, who, now in their early twenties, were finishing college, beginning careers, perhaps marrying and having children of their own—all incredible life transitions of which I could be a part. In addition, I was an easy motorcycle ride away from my parents, who resided near Sacramento and were in their seventies. And, given the Southern California weather, I could motorcycle year-round, including commuting to work at UCLA. The Rock Store chums I acquired were an unanticipated bonus.

But sometimes paradise is not all that you expect it to be. Los Angeles is an international metropolis that offers just about anything you want except decent mass transit, so residents struggle to travel beyond their neighborhoods. I quickly learned that people who live there make no plans without first calculating the pains of traffic to get anywhere, asking themselves such questions as: How far is it? How bad will the traffic be? (Almost always bad, unless it is between midnight and 5:00 am.) Will there be convenient free parking? (Almost never.) Will I be spending three hours in traffic for a one-hour event? Though LA is not alone in the race toward urban dysfunction, it is the leading contender for that Oscar.

Another disadvantage is the weather: although it is never really cold, it can be brutally dry and hot for many months. LA is basically a desert pretending, in Hollywood fashion, to be a tropical land, existing on borrowed and rapidly disappearing water. Add to that LA's distinctive Santa Ana winds. Blowing hot and fierce in late summer and fall from the Mojave Desert, these westward winds sweep through sections of Southern California at speeds not even enjoyed by those on the freeways. Since the coastal terrain is hilly, the winds roar ferociously over the low mountain ridges in their rush to the seaside. Everything not already paved is a tinderbox waiting to explode at the first spark, and sparks come with regularity from careless campers, workmen with power equipment in the hills, or firebugs who seem to enjoy conflagrations. Fall brush fires in Southern California are as predictable as Halloween and Thanksgiving; the only unknowns are the specific hillsides to be scorched each year.

As it turned out, Carol Ann and I, by settling on a high ridge in the Santa Monica Mountains, had unwittingly moved into what is labeled a "burn area." During our second fall, we had to evacuate our house quickly one afternoon as a huge wildfire roared through Malibu Canyon and over a nearby ridge toward our neighborhood. We spent two nights in a hotel room in Santa Monica with our cats, watching live TV coverage of the fire and the aerial bombardment to impede the fury. Many canyon homes were burned; ours and most in our immediate neighborhood were spared. We returned gratefully to a home that we thought we might never see again. However, over the next six years there would be fires almost yearly in the Santa Monica Mountains, some in our canyon within sight of our home. Consequently, our idyllic setting overlooking the ocean lost its serenity, and we reluctantly decided to find a place to live in Southern California where we would not experience high anxiety when the winds blew.

Subsequently, we moved to Ojai, a place I had occasionally explored on riding trips with my buddies. A quaint small town seventy miles north of LA, nestled in a valley of orchards surrounded by mountains, Ojai was generally immune to severe winds and annual fires. Three years after we moved, our former home in the Santa Monica Mountains burned to the ground during a wildfire that destroyed about twenty homes in our old neighborhood, an event that made us thankful we had relocated.

Not so coincidently, our new home in Ojai happened to be situated near the base of Highway 33, a two-lane road running from sea level to five thousand feet through the Los Padres National Forest, considered one of the great motorcycle roads of California. In some ways, I considered Highway 33 the Angeles Crest of Ventura County—a scenic, challenging, risky, fifty-mile thriller—not a bad place for a diehard motorcyclist to live. But there were a few drawbacks I needed to face. First, my round-trip commute to work increased from 50 to 150 miles. Three days a week I spent about three hours on two of the most congested highways in California (the CA101 and I-405), an insane, masochistic commute by any measure that I managed by traveling to work before dawn and lane splitting. The only saving grace was that I was on one of my motorcycles and not in a cage. To counteract the commute, I rode on Saturdays and Sundays for pleasure on the rural roads in the area. I was now an unrepentant rider, motorcycling about 20,000 miles a year. Another drawback was that the Rock Store now was an hour away via the same ridiculous highway I traveled to work. During my early months in Ojai, I continued to frequent the Rock Store but also I began to think about finding some riding compatriots closer to where I lived. Indirectly, a Moto Guzzi Centauro led me in the right direction.

With perhaps the best good fortune that can befall an academic, I was invited in 1995 to spend a month in residence with other scholars from around the world at the Rockefeller Foundation Villa Serbelloni in Bellagio on Lake Como, Italy. My task was to complete a book I was writing (later published as *Making Us Crazy*). By coincidence, my residency in Bellagio overlapped with the annual Milan Motorcycle Show (Esposizione Internazionale Ciclo Motociclo e Accessori), a huge trade show, held for over one hundred years, where manufacturers display their latest creations. Since Milan was a short ferry and train ride from Bellagio, I took a day off to experience the moto extravaganza.

Italy produces some of the most revered and beautiful motorcycles in the world, and although I had never owned an Italian bike they were on my wish list. The venerable Moto Guzzi company, also located near Bellagio, at Mandello de Lario, debuted a new model that year, the Centauro. It was a swoopy roadster, with typical unique Guzzi styling. I was enchanted by the company's display, enhanced by scantily clad models,

and persuaded that this would be my next bike. In
the meantime, while working on my book in Bellagio
I pinned a large poster of the Centauro, which I had
acquired in Milan, in my study. I suspect I have been
the only academic resident at the famed villa to have
ever displayed a large motorcycle poster on its vener-
ated walls.

Several years later, when the Centauro became available in California, I had become slightly less enchanted
with its styling but still very much enthralled with
Guzzis, one of the oldest, if more off-beat, of the Italian
bikes. When Guzzi began selling its V11 Sport, a
model similar to the Centauro, I succumbed. It was
silver with a red frame, on which I mounted a match-
ing Magni fairing for that extra Italian touch. Every
rider has fond memories of bikes owned and sold, but
there is usually at least one sale that causes enduring
remorse; and mine was the eventual sale of my V11
Sport Guzzi, but at least I traded it for another new
Guzzi, a Breva V11 Sport.

The challenge facing an owner of any uncommon
motorcycle is to find a service shop with a knowledge-
able mechanic. A riding buddy suggested I go see David
Blunk at Sport Cycle Pacific in Santa Barbara. He had
exactly what I wanted: a small shop cluttered with
bikes and parts of bikes, an assortment of weird old

motorcycles, and an experienced Guzzi mechanic who rode a Guzzi Quota. It was an ideal place for service and, as I discovered, for hanging out and hearing news of motorcyclist gatherings.

When I began taking my V11 Sport there for service, David mentioned that a periodic gathering of Guzzi riders would be taking place the next Sunday at a café in Ojai. I showed up on time and spotted a small eclectic collection of bikes in the parking lot, including a Guzzi, several Ducati models, and a couple of Beemers. It looked promising. I found a group of riders sitting at an outdoor table, so I introduced myself and joined them. After ordering coffee and breakfast and listening to the friendly, irreverent chatter, I mentioned that David Blunk had suggested I come to this Guzzi gathering. They knew David, and some of them owned Guzzis, but they weren't the Guzzi group, which hadn't arrived yet for breakfast. That group finally arrived a few minutes later and sat at a nearby table. I had mistakenly invited myself for breakfast with the remnants of the older Santa Barbara Italian Motorcycle Group, which by then also included as many riders with non-Italian bikes. Despite the mistake, I remained seated with them, enjoying their company that morning. I was looking for my new niche but did not yet know which group of riders might be for me or would

have me, aware that finding a group can be as troublesome and iffy as dating, except lives are at stake in
group riding. What I did know, from past experience,
was that choosing riding partners was a vital decision
that can affect not only the type of companionship you
have on rides but also safety.

In my ten years of riding out of the Rock Store
with a shifting cadre of riders, I had learned a lot about
riding in groups and how precarious riding safely can
be. Although I had not crashed since my first ride in
Upstate New York over a decade earlier, I had come
upon others who had crashed badly and had witnessed
crashes by those I was accompanying. Almost all these
crashes had been due to rider error, although an occasional car had caused havoc. Fortunately, these crashes
within groups I had joined resulted in damage more
to pride and fairings than to body parts. We had been
very lucky, because we usually traveled at a good clip
and had a string of police citations to prove it.

Riding with strangers was, and still is, unnerving
for me because of not knowing in advance about group
norms, etiquette, or riding idiosyncrasies. With groups
of strangers, there are likely to be vastly different levels
of experience and skills, of common sense, of testosterone and competitiveness, of the need to show off,
demonstrate superior skill, or ride above comfort level
to keep up with the group. Most of the bad motorcycle

crashes I've encountered, a few involving fatalities, were caused by such inclinations within the group.

Even among friends and riding partners it is necessary to guard against unsafe impulses, such as the desire to ride a little faster than usual, perhaps to demonstrate the superiority of some newly purchased model; to chase after some stranger who whizzed by; to pass other bikes or cars in an unsafe manner if they are impeding swift progress; to not slow down in turns when the pavement may be sandy or dirty, or the road unfamiliar. I have had the good fortune of riding with others who did not hesitate to tell me that my passing was perhaps unsafe or that my competitiveness may have gotten the best of me. When friends can critique each other's riding, all riders are safer. Among strangers, however, such critical comments are unlikely—and that's the problem.

Recently, I rode with a large group, mostly strangers. I noticed in the first few miles a young rider making unsafe passes, whose gear consisted of sneakers without socks, jeans, an inadequate jacket, and a helmet for the long day's ride. At the first stop, I mentioned my concerns to the group leader. I suspect no one said anything to the young man. Two hours later he missed a corner and smashed into a fence, incurring minor injuries to his legs. By making riding safety a responsibility, not just for individuals but for the group, accidents are minimized. Such group collaboration builds familiarity and trust among riders.[4]

Ultimately, in another grant of good fortune for me, if not for them, I became a regular of the remnants of Santa Barbara Italian Motorcycle Group. Beginning the next Sunday, and continuing for ten years, I joined them for breakfast every Sunday and for hundreds of rides. These Santa Barbara lads became my new Rock Store regulars.

Like many groups of serious motorcyclists, the Italian Motorcycle Group was an interesting mix of characters who had ridden together for many years. Generally in their forties to sixties, and occasionally including a few women riders, members had the usual wide range of occupations and personal histories. Although most were seasoned riders with roots in California, the group had an international flavor as some members were originally from England, South Africa, New Zealand, and China. I soon discovered that I had infiltrated, although they might say "infested," a group with a long history of memorable rides and

---

[4]The motorcycle literature is full of helpful advice about riding in groups. See, for example, David L. Hough, "Group Riding Tactics," *BMW Motorcycle Magazine* (Winter 2014): 86–88; Peter Egan, "The Fine Art of Riding Your Own Bike," *Cycle World* (July 2006), reprinted in *Leanings* 3 (St. Paul, MN: Motorbooks, 2014); and Nick Ienatsch, "The Pace," *Sport Rider Magazine* (June 1993); http://www.rka-luggage.com/A17%20The%20Pace/thepace.html.

Above the Santa Barbara fog

former illustrious or questionable characters. Their Sunday morning gathering spot was a frontage road along Highway 101 in posh Montecito, adjacent to the railroad tracks and a long-abandoned beach hotel. When all (usually six to twelve regulars) arrived by about 8:00 am, we blasted off to the day's chosen breakfast spot, usually a nice twisty ride away. Whether it was Ojai, Los Olivos, Santa Ynez, or elsewhere, we almost always took the long, crooked route through some part of the Los Padres National Forest. After an outdoor breakfast, we would depart on another ride, usually returning home by early afternoon after a couple hundred miles. When the old hotel was leveled and became a construction site, we changed the meeting spot to Pierre LaFond's, an upscale café a mile away, where we could enjoy a first cup of coffee at the outdoor garden until the laggards arrived for the day's ride.

Most of us owned more than one motorcycle, some many more; and our Sunday rides would occasionally consist of some off-road sections, often following the crest of the mountains surrounding Santa Barbara on West or East Camino Cielo. During these years, I had a garage that housed a changing collection of bikes, which typically included a sport-touring bike with saddlebags for longer overnight trips and commuting, a sport bike for weekend canyon riding, and a smaller dual-sport bike for infrequent dirt rides. Over time we all noted that there were fewer and fewer Italian bikes appearing on Sunday mornings but multiple Beemer GSs and a scattering of Triumphs, Suzuki V-Stroms, and an occasional KTM, Ducati, or Kawasaki, among others.

New riders sometimes joined the group for Sunday rides, and some regulars fell away. A few found the group as I had, through word of mouth or a chance encounter with someone from the group. An exception was Jim, who, with his wife, relocated to Ojai about five years after us. He had been my most steadfast riding buddy from the Rock Store regulars. A lifelong rider and former desert racer, he was a master of the craft. Much of what I had learned about riding skillfully I had learned while chasing him through the canyons of LA and far beyond, and only after many years was I occasionally able to follow him through corners with his swiftness and grace. Within weeks of his move to Ojai, I had Jim coming to the Sunday morning rides. He fit right in as a skilled, diehard motorcyclist accustomed to riding with others, safety conscious, and quick with irreverent quips. A major bonus for me of Jim's relocation was that we were both semiretired and endowed with the famous Highway 33 literally at our doorstep, allowing us at a moment's impulse to get on our bikes and charge up the mountain for lunch at some distant stop, such as Pine Mountain. Weekday rides now became as common as those on weekends.

My decade in Ojai deepened my immersion in motorcycling. The Santa Barbara lads were dedicated riders, always looking for an excuse to plan a long three-hundred- to four- hundred-mile day of riding on back road loops to Lake Isabella in the southern Sierra Nevada Mountains or to San Luis Obispo in central coastal California. On one memorable day ride, we went to lunch at Nepenthe in Big Sur and back home for dinner. These all-day rides, enjoyable as they were, always aroused a tinge of regret—that I had to turn around midday and return home, relinquishing the impulse to keep riding farther away, day after day pursuing a fantasy of the endless ride.

No doubt others felt the same impulse, as the group periodically schemed about taking some days off from work for three- to five-day trips. Depending on the season, the destination might be camping in the Sierra Nevadas or in Death Valley, or a mix of camping and staying in motels. The years were punctuated by such adventures, full of swift riding, good-spirited camaraderie and abundant goofy fun. One of these outings was the annual trip to the Superbike and MotoGP Races at the famed Laguna Seca track in Monterey, California, only a half-day scenic ride from Santa Barbara. A gaggle of the guys and some of their wives, whom we had gotten to know through annual dinners or bizarre gift-giving holiday parties, would stay at cabins at the Ripplewood Inn in Big Sur. We would gather there each evening for dinner, a campfire, and the merriment that comes from telling and retelling tales. To this day, the mention of "but just one goat" will bring hardy laughter as listeners recall a superb tale told by one of the spouses, Karen, around the campfire to a rather inebriated crowd.

Although the Santa Barbara Italian Motorcycle Group lived on long after it had been dominated by Italian bikes and after many of its original members had ceased to ride with the group, no alternative name for the group, or even if it needed a new name, became a topic of discussion—that is, until one of our annual excursions to Death Valley. About a half dozen of us stopped for lunch at Furnace Creek Ranch, where we bought prepared sandwiches and sodas from a small market then sat on steps in the front plaza to enjoy our food. Local vendors were selling trinkets to tourists. One vendor, a pleasant woman selling necklaces, approached each of us suggesting that the items would make wonderful gifts for our wives. Several of us, being cheapskates, declined. But then she had the misfortune of asking Michael, who was not known for being able to subdue his wacky humor. "We don't have wives. We are the Gay Riders Association and Brotherhood," he replied with a straight face. As she was momentarily embarrassed into silence, the rest of us were falling off the stairs in laughter at our insuppressible compatriot. Henceforth, our group had a new informal handle: the Grabbers.

Highway 84, north of Abiquiu, New Mexico

12. New Curves, Dirt Roads— New Mexico

LIFE IS PACKED with decreasing-radius turns. If you are familiar with the road and know the curve ahead, you manage it with skill and grace. But if you're moving too swiftly, not paying attention, or the turn is unexpected, you awkwardly and dangerously run wide. I've tried in life and motorcycling alike to anticipate such tricky corners and come out of them unscathed, with my confidence intact.

I sensed one particular decreasing-radius turn coming years in advance. In January 1986, Carol Ann and I packed her Nissan pickup and drove from Albany, New York, to San Francisco, where we planned to live for six months. On our way to the Left Coast, we stopped in Santa Fe, New Mexico, for two nights. Neither of us had been there or knew much about the quaint four-hundred-year-old Spanish city. It charmed us, and we added it to our list of places to revisit some day.

More than a decade transpired, during which we coped awkwardly with several unexpected sharp turns that took us to New York City then Los Angeles, which offered career opportunities for me. In 1997, we decided to revisit Santa Fe. After spending a week in "The City Different," Carol Ann was smitten. I knew that vacations spent in interesting or glamorous places often stimulate visitors to wonder what it would be like to actually live there, feelings that usually recede with time or subsequent visits. She and I had felt that way when first visiting New York City, Montreal, San Francisco, Bellagio in Italy, and San Miguel de Allende in Mexico. So when it came to Santa Fe I simply suggested that we continue to visit, expecting that in time her fascination would ebb. She made many more visits, and with each one her fascination in fact intensified. She had found her spiritual home. It offered a quieter environment than Southern California and nurtured her interests in arts, crafts, and Spanish culture. Moreover, the vast open landscape made her heart sing.

A decreasing-radius seemed to be just ahead. In her characteristic way, Carol Ann would drop subtle clues about her intentions. She bought an adobe condo near the Santa Fe Plaza to stay in during her visits. She left her Volvo and some clothes in Santa Fe. Then she became a legal resident of New Mexico. I began to sense that only our three cats tied her to California, and they were portable. She obviously had calculated the odds that her moto-crazed husband might be, too.

Eventually, the decreasing-radius turn appeared. We began talking hypothetically about moving to Santa Fe, imagining if, when, and how we might make such a transition, and even entertained the idea of having homes in both places but concluded that two homes would double the headaches and costs and unnecessarily complicate our lives.

Further assessing the situation, I realized that for twenty years my ties to California had been family, employment, and motorcycling friends. My son and daughter in LA were now in their forties, immersed in careers, and married with children. My parents were deceased. My enthusiasm for what had been a very gratifying forty-year career was rapidly waning. Carol Ann had already retired from her career in interior design, and I could retire whenever I wanted. Now in our sixties and in good health, we realized that this might be our last chance to relocate and begin a new chapter of our lives. Although I was content to stay in Ojai, as we had planned when we moved there, Carol Ann had psychologically already left California for New Mexico. She said it was my call.

Coming swiftly down the straightaway, I drifted to the outside, shifted down, lightly squeezed the front brake, and leaned into the inside of the curve, clipping the apex as I accelerated into a new life. It was my turn to follow her, I decided, as she had lovingly followed me around the country. I retired. We sold our house and moved to Santa Fe. I promised my son, daughter, and grandsons that they would see me just as frequently because it took less time to get to their homes by air from Santa Fe than by driving from Ojai to LA in bad traffic. And by leaving a motorcycle with them in LA, during my frequent visits I could also use it to ride north to Santa Barbara for Sunday rides with the Grabbers.

I had no serious concerns about leaving my long career either, or the mild climate of Southern California. When colleagues asked what I was going to do with myself, I told them I honestly didn't know and wasn't worried about it—retirement would be just another adventure in life. But I didn't tell them about my secret retirement bonus, that no longer would my job interfere with riding.

My major concern in relocating was finding new riding friends and discovering a new network of twisty roads. For several years I had explored motorcycling opportunities in New Mexico in preparation for a new moto life. During visits to Santa Fe, I would stop by the BMW shop and schmooze. While at Downtown Subscription, a local coffee café, I would ask motorcyclists about the roads in the vicinity, the riding season, local hangouts, and where they got their bikes serviced. There was often an old Beemer Airhead parked in front of El Mesón, a *tapas* restaurant we frequented, and I quickly made friends with Andrea, the maître d' and Beemer owner. I also clipped articles from motorcycling magazines that featured rides in New Mexico.

In addition, I had made three trips from LA to Santa Fe by motorcycle, once by myself in a four-thousand-mile loop to the Oregon Coast then east through Idaho and south through Utah and Colorado into New Mexico. Twice I invited three Grabbers—Lee, Mike, and Chris—to make a loop with me through Arizona and southern Utah, traveling on as many secondary roads as we could. While each excursion made me realize that nine hundred miles is a long distance from Ojai and a century from the culture of Los Angeles, it also added to my sense of the terrain and byways of the Southwest. And my visits to Santa Fe gave me vital information: there were hundreds of miles of great roads through the mountains and canyons, stunning scenery, and hardly any traffic, ever; I could ride almost year-round; and I could continue to have a full life as a motorcyclist in northern New Mexico. Having made the turn, I now needed to remake my motorcycling life.

I was relieved to end my twenty-year almost daily commute to Los Angeles. But I was saddened to be leaving my weekend rides with the Grabbers. I warned them they weren't getting rid of me so easily, that I would be back to ride with them periodically. And, in fact, I have returned every several months for their Sunday ride, visits that have cushioned my loss as I adjusted to my new environs.

We arrived in New Mexico in the summer of 2013, when the weather was perfect for riding. Having sold three motorcycles in preparation for the move, I needed to acquire an appropriate motorcycle in New Mexico, where a majority of the roads are unpaved. Having for years resisted the pressure to own a Beemer GS, which was the motorcycle of choice among my friends in California, I now sought out a used one on Craigslist. By the time we were unpacked in the new house, I had bought an eight-year-old low-mileage R1200GS. Soon I began making forays into the coun-tryside around Santa Fe, heading north on the High Road to Taos, west into the Jemez Mountains, and south around the Galisteo Basin.

I assumed that I would quickly find groups of motorcyclists strafing the mountain roads on weekend mornings as I had in the mountains near Los Angeles twenty years before. Mimicking my California expe-rience, I would be out riding by 7:00 am on Saturday and Sunday mornings, exploring my new territory and hunting for like-minded motorcyclists. But to my great disappointment the wonderful twisty roads were devoid of motorcyclists and even cars. Although New Mexico is the fifth largest state in geographical size, it has only about two million people scattered across the vast territory and thus little traffic on the roads.

Finding my motorcycling niche in New Mexico required a different strategy than in the past. There was no central gathering spot or destination for weekend riders. At one time Café at Dawn, near Albuquerque, was such a venue but only on late Sunday mornings during good weather. And by the time I discovered this the café had closed permanently. I noticed that there was a substantial riding community of Harley-Davidson owners, and undoubtedly in Albuquerque, they had some hangouts, but that was unlikely to be my niche; there were no Harleys or even cruisers among the thirty bikes I had owned over the years. Nevertheless, I kept seeing a number of Beemers on the roads around Santa Fe, and I figured there must be active motorcyclists in town.

I emailed my Ojai riding buddy, Jim, about my early failures. Within a day, he sent me a link to a website he had found for a sport-touring riding group in Santa Fe called Pegasus. Pegasus had been founded by Zeo (aka Peter), a Brooklyn exile who had organized

a loose collection of sport riders several years before
my arrival in New Mexico and posted e-mail alerts for
group rides every several weeks. I joined the group
online and awaited notice of their next ride.

Subsequently, an alert was posted for a Sunday
ride leaving at 10:00 am from Rio Rancho, forty minutes from my house. The riding destination for the
day was east and north via Highway 4 into the Jemez
Mountains, a road I had ridden only once. A group
of about six riders showed up at the designated gas
station at 10:00 am, which seemed like a late start
for a summer ride since by late morning I had often
already traveled one hundred miles. It was an eclectic
assortment of young and older riders with a mix of
bikes, including a new Kawi 300, an Aprilia thumper,
a Ducati 900SS, a Versys, and my older GS. We headed
for the nearby mountains and, after about thirty
miles, rode up a narrow canyon, where we stopped,
dismounted, and chatted for about thirty minutes. It
was an opportunity for me to discover that, among
this small pleasant group, one guy was originally from
San Diego while another, Massimo, riding the Ducati,
had lived in Santa Clarita, California, and had a familiar license frame from Pro Italia (a well-known Ducati
shop in LA). Massimo and I had both ridden the same
famous canyon roads in Southern California, such as
the Angeles Crest, and I had also once owned a Ducati

like the one he was riding. I was relieved to know that there were sport bike riders in the area with whom I could find some common ground.

I was concerned, however, because it was now past 11:00 am and our tires weren't even warm yet. Following another short stop, I got impatient. I enjoyed the camaraderie but preferred to ride rather than talk. I offered some lame excuse, left the group, and continued alone, going north on Highway 4 heading back to Santa Fe. After five miles on a wonderfully curvy road, Massimo, who had also apparently checked out on the others, came up fast behind me, and I waved him through. This was more like it. Here was a former California rider who rode in an enthusiastic and skilled California way. Unable to resist, I sped up to get to a safe but sporting distance behind him as we navigated a sequence of challenging turns. We were clipping along at 65 to 75 mph, a swift but controlled pace that was both familiar and deeply satisfying. There was good, dry pavement, little traffic, and a beautiful mountain highway that stretched for fifty miles. I had no problem hanging with him, not after chasing my Ojai friend Jim and others for twenty years in the canyons of California. Here was a rider I could dance with. But after about four miles he signaled a left turn on the road to Fenton Lake, the next established spot for the Pegasus group to stop and chat. I waved good-bye

and continued straight on my way back to Santa Fe.
Once again I was riding alone. Nevertheless, this spurt
of spirited riding had given me the sense that I might
have found a connection to the riding community in
New Mexico.

Consequently, I was feeling good as I advanced
north toward the Valles Caldera. I had unexpectedly
discovered the caldera, the result of a huge volcanic
eruption 1.2 million years ago and now a national preserve, a week before, riding from the opposite direction.
I had crested a mountain ridge west of Los Alamos and
descended into a giant, grass-covered mountain basin
thirteen miles wide, cut through by a river, surrounded
by mountain peaks and old-growth forests, and inhab-
ited by herds of elk and other magnificent wildlife. I
was awestruck by the beauty of the vast landscape; it
was as if I had unknowingly come upon the edge of the
Grand Canyon or Yosemite Valley.[5]

Now in high spirits and just minutes away from
sweeping past the southern edge of the gorgeous caldera, I found the scenery magnificent, the weather
perfect, the twisting highway divine, the expanses
of meadows and evergreen forests captivating. I was

[5]For an engaging review of the geological, political, and social
history of this area, see William deBuys and Don J. Usner, *Valles
Caldera: A Vision for New Mexico's National Preserve* (Santa Fe, NM:
Museum of New Mexico Press, 2006).

eagerly anticipating the forty more miles of this glorious road, enthralled by the experience. It was one of those riding moments that makes the hearts of motorcyclists sing, gives meaning to our humble lives, makes us deeply appreciate being alive.

Then I noticed that someone else seemed to be appreciating the day, too. In my rearview mirror were flashing red lights from an apparently excited car driver. I pulled over for a friendly chat with an official representative from the state of New Mexico. He was so impressed with my superior riding that he awarded me a certificate of achievement. I swelled with pride at this official award, despite having moved to New Mexico only a month before.

As my conversation with the officer soon revealed, when I had traded my California driver's license for a New Mexico one, the new license, unbeknownst to me, had not included the additional endorsement needed to ride motorcycles. Since I was not legally licensed to ride a motorcycle in New Mexico, he surprised me with a second certificate of achievement and an invitation to visit the Magistrate's Courthouse in Bernalillo County within the week. Welcome to New Mexico, I thought.

Later I couldn't resist sharing the good news with my riding buddies in California. A few skeptics suggested that I enlist a team of New York lawyers to help with the paperwork, financing, and public relations.

Entering New Mexico from Colorado

But New Mexico isn't that kind of state. It's very low key. Ultimately, I humbly accepted the commendations, had friendly chats with the court clerk, got a call at home from the judge, exchanged a little cash for the commendations, and nothing appeared in my driving records. Then I got a brand-new motorcycle license and continued riding. When I told Jim, he replied, "Where do you live, Mayberry?" I smiled at the possible resemblance between Santa Fe and the fictional TV sitcom town known for its low crime rate. I now look for Officer Friendly whenever I ride past the caldera, but he hasn't awarded me any commendations since then. I think it was a newcomer's special.

As I continued to search for my motorcyclist niche in New Mexico, the Pegasus group, with its frequent announced rides, provided a changing mix of men and women riders. In addition to Massimo, I met Peter and India, new transplants from the San Francisco Bay Area, who were very good riders in the mode of my former California riding friends, and Richard, a recently retired owner of a motorcycle and scooter shop in Santa Fe, who knew just about everyone in the local motorcycle community. These were riders I was to see repeatedly at various venues in my early years in Santa Fe.

The local Santa Fe BMW shop also occasionally sponsored group rides, both on- and off-road, and I tried to participate in each one at first. They were usually all-day outings on interesting loops in the mountains, involving several dozen men and women representing the aging Beemer demographic, who had varying levels of skill and experience. Such a mixture always posed a risk of mishaps but nevertheless proved to be another entry into the New Mexico riding community.

Additionally, I serendipitously discovered a hub of activity for Beemer and vintage bike owners when other riders suggested that I contact a master mechanic named Marc Beyer. Marc and his partner, Frances, had recently opened their own service shop,

OCD Custom Cycles & Repair.[6] I found the shop one day and dropped in to look it over. I was familiar with the corporate slickness of many new BMW motorcycle franchises, with their front showrooms of new bikes and separate sections for apparel and accessories, and service departments hidden in the rear. Marc's shop was a striking contrast. There were funky posters on the wall, a collection of Marc's racing trophies, and no showroom or new motorcycles, but a captivating vintage bike ambience and an array of dismantled bikes of all brands and ages on the lifts. It was as if I had stepped into the personal garage of a true bike mechanic and aficionado, infused with the wholesome smell of grease. I knew immediately that I had found my mechanic and discovered that the shop was a meeting place for Beemer and vintage bike owners. Even during my early visits it was common to encounter friends there or recognize their bikes on the lifts. As a result of all this, OCD Custom Cycles & Repair quickly became my replacement for David Blunk's Sport Cycle Pacific in Santa Barbara, where I would always find friends hanging around. Finding a good shop was as important to me as finding a good cardiologist is to a heart patient.

---

[6]For more information about Marc Beyer, see James Parker, "Apprentice to Master," *Motorcyclist Magazine* (July 2015): 26.

Another tip I received for finding the motorcycling community came from both Richard and Marc and involved a group of sport bike riders who occasionally met on Sunday mornings at the Santa Fe Baking Company and Café. The Bakery Café group, organized by Luis, sent an alert about a proposed ride every week or so in riding weather. The younger men and women in this group, I was to learn, rode at a brisk pace on the captivating twisty highways around Santa Fe and Albuquerque.

It was on my first BMW shop ride, billed as a relatively easy GS off-road excursion, that my motorcycling life expanded to a new arena. Other than the shop staff, I knew no one among the thirty people participating in this ride, which was to be my first off-road ride in my new state on my new-to-me GS. So I double checked with the staff several days before the ride to get reassurance that even newbie dirt riders like me, straddling big GSs, could manage the terrain without too much anxiety. On the day of the ride, we meandered for several hours in the hills and arroyos south and east of Santa Fe on unpaved ranch roads. We then paused before lunch in a park near the village of Villanueva. There I pulled out my map and, struggling to understand the geography of my new terrain, asked other riders if they knew exactly where we were. The first few guys I asked were as disoriented as I was.

Then I approached a tall, stately fellow in full Klim gear, Randy, who was standing next to his fully tricked-out F800GS. He not only knew where we were but pulled out a detailed forest map of the entire Santa Fe area. A semiretired attorney from Houston who had moved to Santa Fe two years before me, Randy had only been riding for about a decade but had already ridden all over the country and on most continents. On his map he pointed at the forest roads in the surrounding mountains and said he intended to ride all of them but not on the GS. He had recently purchased a Yamaha WR250R dual-sport bike specifically for dirt riding, and he was eager to begin. Being appropriately reluctant to ride isolated forest roads alone, he surprisingly suggested that I buy a small dual-sport bike and join him in riding this vast network of forest roads. Was he serious? I had just met him; we knew almost nothing about each other or even about our riding styles. On the other hand, here was a person who was as passionate about motorcycling as I. I said I would think about it.

Subsequently, Randy helped me complete the quest to find my motorcycling niche in New Mexico. Spontaneously offering to show me some of his favorite paved roads in northern New Mexico, he arranged a spectacular three-hundred-mile loop to Mora, Angel Fire, the Rio Grande Gorge, and back to Santa Fe—by any measure, superb riding territory. Moreover, I discovered that we traveled at a similar pace, needed to stop at similar intervals, and were comfortable spending most of our time riding rather than stopping.

I then confronted the new challenge of riding on dirt. Randy continued to ask me periodically if I was going to get a small dual-sport bike and ride on back roads with him. In response, I began to read reviews and comparisons of 250cc dual-sport bikes and visited motorcycle shops, finally deciding to buy a Honda CBF250L because of its excellent reviews and, more importantly, because the seat was low enough for my feet to reach the ground. The positioning of my feet was critical since I had limited experience riding on dirt and felt considerable anxiety about launching this off-roading adventure.

As soon as I acquired the Honda in mid-January, Randy was prepared to begin exploring the dirt roads just southwest of Santa Fe and within a few miles of where we each lived; we would save the mountain forest roads for late spring and summer. As weather permitted, we began riding around Sage Brush Flats and Caja del Rio Plateau, exploring new unpredictable dirt roads through the Santa Fe National Forest. In the process, I received a full introduction to crossing sand-filled arroyos, picking my way through stretches of rocky terrain, and quickly diagnosing the risks of careening along roads creased by deep muddy ruts.

Every mile of rough road challenged my natural instincts about riding. Many of the skills I had carefully honed over twenty years on pavement did not pertain to riding on dirt. Instead of decelerating when the tires began slipping around, I had to accelerate. Bumpy roads were made smoother not by going slower but by speeding up. More control was gained not by tucking into the bike and countersteering but by standing upright on the pegs and thus lowering the center of gravity. Each time out I was an experienced street rider feeling like a complete newbie; however, with Randy's encouragement I persevered. Before the riding season was over that fall, I had covered over a thousand miles on local dirt roads. My anxiety had diminished, and my confidence had grown, although my skills had only increased to rudimentary levels. Uneven terrain now caused me little concern: I could traverse gravel roads with relative ease and overcome brief encounters with deep sand. I had gained great satisfaction from learning something new and exploring a different facet of motorcycling.

This initial training resulted in many other benefits. One was meeting the many serious riders Randy introduced me to, who provided me with additional connections to like-minded riders in Santa Fe. During my first autumn, I was invited to join Pascal, Alain, David, and Randy on a fall GS ride to the Monument

Valley area of southern Utah, which included a few days of on- and off-road riding amidst spectacular scenery. The following year I joined this group several times for local dirt rides and later for a week of dirt riding near Apache Lake in Arizona. The most memorable experience of that trip was riding a rugged and challenging forty-five-mile stretch of the Backcountry Discovery Route along Cherry Creek Road up to the town of Young and living to tell about it. These guys, all experienced riders, both on and off road, patiently tolerated my novice status in dirt riding.

Another benefit was that Randy was an avid long-distance rider and needed no coaxing to undertake multiday trips. During my first spring, we took our Beemers and headed to Arizona for a week, where we rode on twisty empty roads through small towns and hilly terrain from Sedona and Flagstaff in the north to Bisbee in the southeast, with only an occasional massive strip-mining site to mar the otherwise attractive southwestern landscape.

A few months later I mentioned to Randy that I needed to see some elderly relatives in Lethbridge, Alberta, and was planning to ride there in August. He quickly asked if he could join me on the excursion. We plotted a tentative route that would allow us to ride as many great motorcycle roads as possible going north through Colorado, Idaho, Wyoming, and Montana and then different roads going back home. Over nine days, we had magnificent riding through the Rockies. Except for one afternoon ride into a serious thunderstorm in Wyoming, during which I saw my first tornado spinning in the clouds above us, the weather was perfect and the journey nearly flawless. We encountered the usual glimpses of wildlife in such terrain: a bear crossing the road, fields of elk and antelope, and so forth. The most enduring experience was riding across a desolate, high mesa in Wyoming one afternoon. Spotting some animals on the highway far ahead in an area of open range, I expected that they were cattle, but when we stopped less than a hundred yards away we realized they were a small herd of female wild mustangs and their colts. They casually stepped a few yards to the side of the road, allowing us to pass and leaving us with the memory of a rare event that we would treasure.

These riding experiences during my first two years in New Mexico on dirt roads and small byways of the southwestern and mountain states reassured me that my new moto life was emerging. Not only did they eradicate any residual uncertainties I had about retiring and moving, but they bolstered my confidence in my riding future.

When I began my life as a serious motorcyclist, I was in my mid-forties. As I settled into New Mexico, I turned seventy, now a grateful, if bewildered, recipient of senior discounts and social security. Still, I hoped my future as a motorcyclist would include many more new challenges, including an array of decreasing-radius turns and the refined ability to take life's curves at full speed, leaning in.

Heading into Montana from Idaho

13. See You in Missoula

Motorcycling as a State of Mind

FOLLOWING **MY** **REENTRY** into motorcycling, my many years of riding—first learning skills, then finding my niche in the sport, in both California and New Mexico, and finally transitioning from riding as training to riding for enjoyment—led to a new comprehension of how motorcycling can reflect a state of mind. This realization dawned during a special nine-day trip to Montana. It was Saturday the Fourth of July, and I awoke well before daybreak in anticipation of the trip, adrenaline replacing my need for caffeine. I would be riding with the same men I had ridden with on an earlier trip to Colorado, only this time our rendezvous site was an all-night café in the San Fernando Valley, where we were to be gassed up and ready to go. As I rode toward the coast, the cool, salty night air triggered memories of that prior long trip.

The riders I was meeting included interesting characters in their fifties, like me, whom I had met years
before as Rock Store regulars. Jim was an Anthony
Hopkins look-alike who rode with the mastery of a
guru, reflecting his former status as a desert racer.
Ryan was a tall serial jokester and a successful entrepreneur who relished this kind of middle-of-the-night
excursion and needed to ride like a junkie craves a fix,
to soothe an unsettled soul. Joel was an impeccably
outfitted manager of a car dealership who considered
each squashed bug on his highly polished black Beemer
a personal insult. David was a book connoisseur and
director of a private library who was abandoning his
buttoned-down job for a week of riding. And I was a
mild-mannered, bearded university professor dressed
in worn leathers, smiling like an excited schoolboy
about to play hooky.

Our purported destination was Missoula, Montana,
for a national Beemer rally. But Montana was not really
our destination, nor was attending the rally our real
purpose. They were the pretext for a road trip; the
excuse to not schedule business meetings for a week
and be officially unavailable by phone or fax; the ruse
to replace our overregulated lives with the unstructured
freedom of a motorcycle trip, riding on roads new to us
where each morning we had no idea where we would
sleep that night. It was to be four thousand miles of fun.

We headed north up the California coast to Oregon and Washington and into Idaho and Montana in search of the longest and most enticing route. But we didn't have the slightest need to know where that route would take us each day. Our sole task was to seek the best roads and stay off the interstate highways with their hordes of summer travelers in RVs. For example, on our second day traveling in northern California the roads through the coastal mountains around Mendocino were so spectacular that we traversed them three times, careening along on three different twisty roads between the cool, overcast coastline and the baking heat of the inland valleys. Among this road-hardened group, I was dubbed the canary in the mine because when I wilted at the end of the day it was time for everyone to stop.

The weather was glorious for riding, cool enough in the early mornings to use our electric vests yet warm enough in the afternoons to wear only T-shirts under unzipped leathers. Although storms were moving across the northwest, we'd had no rain in nine days, miraculously managing to ride between storms. We rose at dawn every day and rode a hundred miles before breakfast. Each day offered its own delights: the northern California coast with its majestic redwood groves; the mountains in central Oregon, which we also crossed three times; the high-rolling plains of southeastern Washington; and the Rocky Mountains and meadows of Idaho and western Montana.

In keeping with the spirit of the ride, we didn't stop much. My few photos show our motorcycles parked at gas stations, cafés, and motels, not because those stops were particularly memorable but because those were the only times I could pull my camera out of the saddlebag. The essence of the road trip could not have been captured in photos anyway because it consisted of numerous experiences and stories that could only be related verbally and shared in person.

Road trips create their own unexpected story lines for the participants, made up of dozens of shared incidents. These add to the lore of the trip, become opportunities for humor and exaggeration, and transform the ride into more than mere travel. For example, at one stop in northern California, Ryan asked if we had seen the two elk standing, as if staged, on the side of the road in a redwood forest just beyond the warning sign that read, "Watch for Elk Crossing." The rest of us had seen nothing, an unsettling reminder of how vulnerable riders are to hazards and their limited capacity to spot them all. Ryan wondered how we could have missed the elk since they were pretty big hazards to miss and asked what had we expected— for the beasts to have flashing red warning lights on their antlers?

Highway 1, northern California coast

Somewhere just south of Eugene, Oregon, clipping along at about 90 mph, our guru Jim lost his wallet, having left a pocket unzipped in his Aerostitch after a gas stop. Our master rider was a victim of his own haste and now completely dependent on us—for gas, meals, and motels—for the remainder of the trip. The irony was not lost. Jim began referring to himself as the "sponsored rider," and we kept reminding him that he should not ride so fast as to lose us, as he usually did, because without our credit cards his ride was finished. We also joked about the imagined hitch-hiker who, stumbling along the highway, had probably found Jim's wallet and was comfortably seated on the

Concorde on his way to a wild Parisian vacation at our guru's expense.

Our stop at a tiny hamburger shack in a forest at the Oregon border taught us a lesson about discovering simple great cuisine in the backcountry. A local couple, learning we were previously from LA, asked us if we knew about the Rock Store. "We *are* the Rock Store," Ryan exclaimed, smiling at his recollections of the place that was informally our second home.

Running out of gas in the middle of nowhere became a painful lesson about the necessity for careful planning, even for unstructured travel. All these incidents became lasting memories of the trip, reminding us of our shared experience and our interdependence.

We were all traveling the same interesting roads, facing the same risks, seeing the same stunning scenery, sharing the common joy of riding, and moving at the same restless pace. Yet in a fundamental way we were riding alone, confined in protective gear, on our own moto, and in our own reality. Unlike traveling in a car, motorcycling with a small group combines elements of separateness and togetherness. On this trip, after a stop for gas or food, and brief conversations as we mounted our bikes, the departing refrain to one another—originated by our guru—was, "See you in Missoula." This farewell expression was not an indication that we might not see each other until we arrived in Montana. Missoula, in this case, did not refer to a specific geographical destination but instead reflected our recognition that when we commenced riding we would each be riding alone yet also together by virtue of sharing a certain state of mind through riding. Like most motorcyclists, I have a drawer full of T-shirts acquired at rallies, races, and dealerships. My favorite T-shirt reads, across the front, "Motorcycling: More Than Just a Sport" and, in small letters on the back, "A State of Mind." The essence of the sport of motorcycling is achieving this elusive state of mind.

Roads across the country inspire this state of mind. They have in common magnificent scenery, smooth pavement, and a series of perfectly arced curves known as fast sweepers. Fast sweepers are paradoxical: gentle, easy, perfectly shaped curves that entice riders to travel at far greater speeds, evoking a sensation of soaring, they demand deft, flowing, totally controlled action. Motorcycles, like airplanes, defy gravity through speed by delicately balancing opposing physical forces; this elusive balance, like a wavering tipping point, suspends the speeding leaned-over rider. In fast sweepers, where the tenuous equilibrium must be sustained longer in gravity-defying flight, riders traveling very fast have a sense of flying low over the landscape. Their bodies are an intricate part of the machine-in-motion, and their sensitive control of the throttle can adjust the altitude a fraction of an inch through the broad turn. Fast sweepers are certainly about speed and control, yet they are also about contemplation and grace.

Fast sweepers are both ominous and treasured. The risks of speed, however, are in abeyance as riders confidently accept that they and their machines are bound together in a controlled motion carrying them along an irrevocable arc of sensation. Moto journalists often describe a bike's ability to handle corners "as if on a rail." The railroad metaphor evokes the sense of being on a fixed, secure trajectory, of having the experience precisely programmed, of requiring nothing more than submission to the flow.

Fast sweepers are the blank canvases awaiting the masterpieces of riding that can result in the state of mind possible while motorcycling. Such challenges demand a deep faith in self and circumstance. You cannot experience them if your mind is elsewhere or if you dwell on the obvious risks. As you cling to the contour of the motorcycle, nestled within the rumbling of its pistons and gears, cradled by its suspension, you seek to be in perfect harmony with the machine. While the world is reeling by, you flirt with the illusion that you and machine are seemingly motionless.

The best fast sweepers—always amidst magnificent scenery—induce an altered sense. You don't *see* the details of the environment, but you become acutely attuned to the changing temperature of the air in the shade of a mountain, the aroma of meadow grasses, and the hiss of air splitting. Being leaned over at speed shifts your place in the landscape. Just as you are enfolded in your bike, you also fuse with your surroundings, feeling momentarily part of the meadow, rolling hills, tilted sky, or swirling stream carving a canyon. You are like an atom whose motion has no precise location, only an undefined presence.

The first time I succumbed to fast sweepers was on Highway 89 riding east from Burlington, Vermont, toward New Hampshire, where as a novice rider traveling over 90 mph, I was giving in to impulses I didn't understand. Years later it would happen to me on Highway 33 north out of Ojai; on the Angeles Forest Highway; north from Cambria on Highway 1 toward Big Sur; and more recently, on Highway 84 north of Georgia O'Keeffe's home in Abiquiu, New Mexico, all 100 miles to Colorado. The road we took heading into Montana that crisp mountain morning was also one of these. It was a road I had never traveled, and it came as an unexpected gift. As the road and vista opened up, so did our throttles. The road and landscape have an immediate presence to a motorcyclist—they are rushing inches below your feet, filling your senses with color, smells, and sounds. As your speed increases, your immediate surroundings blur, but trying to focus on any one aspect in your visual field is a distraction from the larger task and thus an invitation to disaster. As my buddies and I were crossing into Montana—a state of dusty roads and severe weather, an unlikely setting for a flying ballet of motion—the wide sweeping road summoned, and I, as if in a trance, twisted the throttle to catch the horizon. The landscape began morphing into a blur of colors, and the dashed center line became a pulsing streak at my feet as I melded into the machine, gliding above the smooth pavement. My many years and miles of struggling to master the complexities of motorcycling slipped away in the wind. In this moment, as speed increased, there was no thinking about the contact patch, the subtleties of counter-steering, or the physics of motion. The road, setting, and motorcycle were transporting me to a different state of mind: a place where speed is incidental, where risk is subdued by artistry, and where motion is poetry. Suspended in the air and from self-consciousness, I felt serenely at one with my place in this world.

My friends, I'll see you in Missoula.

ABOUT THE AUTHOR

STUART A. KIRK recently retired as a distinguished professor of social welfare at the University of California, Los Angeles, where his academic research focused on the interplay of science, social values, and professional politics in the helping professions. He is the coauthor or author of nine books, many chapters, and over one hundred articles published in social welfare, psychology, psychiatry, and other journals. Among his books are *Science and Social Work: A Critical Appraisal*; *The Selling of DSM: The Rhetoric of Science in Psychiatry*; *Making Us Crazy: DSM—The Psychiatric Bible and the Creation of Mental Disorders*; and *Mad Science: Psychiatric Coercion, Diagnosis, and Drugs*, which have been translated into French, Italian, and Japanese. He has also published op-ed columns in the *New York Times*, the *Los Angeles Times*, and *Newsweek* magazine.

A psychiatric social worker early in his career, Professor Kirk served on President Carter's Commission on Mental Health Task Panel on Deinstitutionalization, Rehabilitation, and Long-Term Care, and evaluated programs designed for those with severe behavioral problems in several states. He was dean of the School of Social Welfare at the State University of New York at Albany and a professor at Columbia University School of Social Work before joining the Department of Social Welfare at UCLA, where he served as director of the PhD program for eight years and as chair of the department for three years.

In 2003, he received the annual award for Significant Lifetime Achievement from the Council on Social Work Education. In 2010, he was inducted as a fellow into the American Academy of Social Work and Social Welfare, an honor society of distinguished scholars.

Professor Kirk resides in Santa Fe, New Mexico, with his wife, three cats, and four motorcycles.